Big Flavor from Small Kitchens

COMPACT COOKING

JENNA HUNTER, MS, RD

Lovingly dedicated to my family, my friends, and my supporters on social media. Thank you all for the endless love and support. I do this for you, and I love you all!

First published in 2023 by Fremont Press

Copyright © 2023 Jenna Hunter

ISBN-13: 978-1-628605-35-8

The information included in this book is for educational purposes only. It is not intended or implied to be a substitute for professional medical advice. The reader should always consult their healthcare provider to determine the appropriateness of the information for their own situation or if they have any questions regarding a medical condition or treatment plan. Reading the information in this book does not constitute a physician-patient relationship.

Cover design by Kat Lannom

Interior design and illustrations by Yordan Terziev and Boryana Yordanova

Lifestyle photography by Johanna Jones

Additional food photography by Crizalie Olimpo, Elita San Juan, and Charisse Reyes

Printed in Canada

TC 0224

INTRODUCTION

Hello, and welcome to your new best friend, *Compact Cooking*. If you are currently living in a dorm room, hotel room, or efficiency apartment without kitchen appliances, or you have unreliable appliances that break down frequently, then this is the cookbook for you. It includes balanced and nutritious meals that you can make using compact appliances such as air fryers, slow cookers, toaster ovens, microwaves, and hot plates.

Not only will this book make your cooking life easier, but it will help you become more efficient at creating nourishing meals on a budget and when you're short on time. You can even take these recipes on the go for camping, tailgating, and other outdoor activities.

MY STORY

You may be wondering how I came to write a book about cooking meals with compact appliances. Well, I'm a dietitian who loves to connect with people through food, but there's more to it than that. During my time as an undergraduate dietetics student at West Virginia University and later as I worked on my master's and doctorate degrees, I became determined to cook and nourish my body to the best of my ability. However, I first lived in a dorm room with no kitchen appliances other than a mini-fridge and a microwave. Then I lived in apartments with old appliances that would break every month. And of course, as a student, I was on a tight budget and had limited time to cook, so I found it challenging not to rely on premade meals and fast food. That was when I turned to the microwave, air fryer, slow cooker, and toaster oven for making budget-friendly and quick-to-prepare meals and snacks.

Cooking has been a hobby of mine since childhood. I began helping my parents in the kitchen when I was eight years old. I remember the first thing we made as a family: chocolate chip and oat cookies. I still make that recipe today. The experiences of cooking with my parents are the reason I became a dietitian.

I also would watch food and cooking videos on YouTube before I went to sleep. (I still do that.) As I watched, I'd think about how interesting it would be to have a fun hobby of filming myself while I cooked and then editing and posting the videos, but I never expected to become a person who would do something like that.

When we were all staying home at the start of the pandemic, I had a lot of free time. It seemed like a great time to start something new, such as cooking and posting videos to social media, just like the creators I had watched when I was younger. That is when The Healthy Hophead was born. The name was inspired by my first pet bunny, Cookie. When she was a baby, she would hop around like she'd just drunk ten energy shots. I used to call her my little hoppy head. So, when it came time to name my socials, I decided to honor her memory.

Since then, I believe I have perfected the art of cooking with small appliances and minimal ingredients. Even today, whenever I'm too busy to make a meal or lack the energy to cook a complicated dish and clean up afterward, I refer to these recipes. I hope you find them as helpful as I do!

ALL ABOUT A BALANCED DIET

Balance: it's the key to true health and wellness. When it comes to food, eating the rainbow and having a good balance among carbs, proteins, and fats are the key elements to exceptional health.

No single food meets all human needs. Our bodies require a variety of nutrients—including plenty of fat-soluble vitamins, water-soluble vitamins, and minerals—that come from an array of foods, and all foods fit into a well-balanced diet. For example, we need fruits and vegetables to meet our fiber, vitamin, and mineral needs. Meats and legumes are excellent sources of iron and protein. Dairy and fortified nondairy products provide the micronutrient calcium, which we need for bone health. A balanced diet can help prevent nutrition-related diseases such as diabetes, heart disease, high blood pressure, and even some forms of cancer.

Furthermore, if you are prone to disordered eating, a balanced diet is best because it does not require you to restrict any foods or food groups, nor are foods labeled "good" or "bad." With your meals and snacks, it is always best to aim for variety so you're giving your body all the nutrients it needs to function properly and for you to feel your best. I created this cookbook with recipes that can help you meet all your nutrient needs while being mindful of the time and labor involved.

Some of the recipes in this book make great well-balanced meals. Others, such as some in the snack and desserts chapters, are weighted more heavily toward some macronutrients than others—most often carbohydrates. I have included protein powder in many of those recipes to increase the protein content and help offset the carbs.

But remember, healthy and well-balanced doesn't have to mean flavorless or boring. I'll be the first to admit that I'm a dietitian with a sweet tooth! That is why I have included some of my favorite sweet breakfasts and desserts in this book. Even though they may have a high sugar content, they are single servings that can be part of a balanced diet when eaten in moderation.

Lastly, I have included a large number of poultry dishes because chicken and turkey are excellent sources of lean and affordable protein. The same is true of fish, which contains heart-healthy omega-3 fats. There are also plenty of vegetarian options for those of you who prefer to eat some meatless meals or avoid meat altogether. And I've included a few beef recipes for when you're craving a hearty red-meat meal, although I tend to eat red meat only occasionally.

WHAT IS COMPACT COOKING?

You may be wondering what compact cooking is, exactly. Compact cooking is all about making meals, desserts, and snacks using small appliances, such as air fryers, slow cookers, microwaves, and toaster ovens. This way of cooking is perfect for people who live in apartments or houses with minimal or no cooking appliances, and for people who prefer not to use their full-sized ovens or find that using compact appliances is more efficient. For example, I don't like using my oven during the summer. Therefore, I often use my toaster oven to cook meals on hot days. After a long workday or when I am otherwise too busy to cook a meal and do a lot of cleanup afterward, I line my air fryer with some aluminum foil or parchment paper and cook a quick meal.

HOW TO USE THIS BOOK

Most of the recipes in this book are quite simple, and they all serve one to four people; many of them yield just one or two servings. If you are not a fan of leftovers, these smaller-yield recipes will help you reduce food waste. However, if you do like leftovers or love the convenience of cooking once and eating twice (or three or four times!), I've provided directions for storage and reheating.

In addition, many of the recipes are versatile in terms of the preparation method—you may be able to use a regular oven or toaster oven, the stovetop or a hot plate, or an air fryer or toaster oven/regular oven. I've included icons to indicate which appliance(s) can be used for each recipe. Additional icons identify which special diets the recipes are appropriate for—vegetarian, vegan, and/or gluten-free—and whether the recipes contain common allergens (dairy, eggs, nuts, and/or peanuts). In many cases I suggest modifications at the end of a recipe to make it vegan, gluten-free, dairy-free, and so on.

For convenience, I have organized the recipes into five chapters: Simple Breakfasts, Effortless Lunches, Satisfying Snackies, Easy-Peasy Dinners, and Sweet Treats. Some of the chapters are further divided into sections; for example, there are both sweet and savory breakfasts, and the dinner chapter includes a section of quick-to-prepare recipes and another of recipes that take a little longer to make.

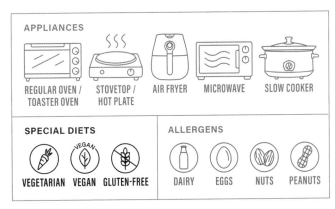

APPLIANCES

REGULAR OVEN / TOASTER OVEN — STOVETOP / HOT PLATE — AIR FRYER — MICROWAVE — SLOW COOKER

SPECIAL DIETS

VEGETARIAN — VEGAN — GLUTEN-FREE

ALLERGENS

DAIRY — EGGS — NUTS — PEANUTS

COMPACT COOKING APPLIANCES

In this section, I'll introduce you to my go-to compact cooking appliances. These handy tools make preparing nutritious home-cooked meals possible in even the most limited kitchen setups. I've included some of my favorite tips and tricks for using them, such as how to cook the perfect egg in an air fryer or microwave and how to cook pasta in a microwave (it's so much faster than waiting for a large pot of water to come to a boil on the stovetop!).

AIR FRYER

There are two types of air fryers: the basket type and the oven type. I use a 6.8-quart Cosori Dual Blaze Smart Air Fryer, which is a basket type, but you can use an oven type to make the recipes in this book. To be concise, in the recipe instructions I refer only to the air-fryer basket. If yours has a tray, simply use that instead. Make sure to use oven- and microwave-safe dishes when air-frying foods.

I like the Cosori air fryer because it has a large basket and multi-purpose buttons for cooking fish, chicken, fries, and more. It even includes defrosting and reheating buttons. Similar air fryers that work exceptionally well are the PowerXL Vortex Air Fryer and the Philips Air Fryer Essential Collection. I find that these types of air fryers work best for cooking or reheating foods, and you do not need to preheat them. Other models may need to be preheated, so make sure to check the user manual for your particular model.

For easy cleanup, line your air-fryer basket or tray with parchment paper or aluminum foil. In many cases you can use either, but I find that foil works better for air-frying meat and fish.

COOKING TIPS

EGGS: Make soft-boiled eggs by air-frying at 360°F for six minutes. For a hard-boiled egg, increase the time to ten minutes. To scramble eggs, line the air-fryer basket or tray with parchment paper or greased aluminum foil. Crack the eggs over the lined basket or tray and lightly beat with a whisk or fork. Air-fry at 360°F for seven minutes.

SANDWICHES: When air-frying sandwiches, use toothpicks so the top slice of bread doesn't fly off.

REHEATING FOOD: The air fryer is great for reheating breaded foods or foods that were previously baked because it maintains their crispiness. You can reheat food in an air fryer at 350°F for one to three minutes.

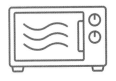

MICROWAVE

A microwave that has a wattage of 800 to 1,000 works best for these recipes. When microwaving foods, I like to use medium-high to high power for a shorter cooking time. The microwave does not need to have special functions; it only needs to have Start and Stop buttons and a keypad for setting the time.

COOKING TIPS

EGGS: Eggs can't be microwaved in their shells because the yolks will explode. Instead, crack the eggs into a microwave-safe bowl and whisk them (or beat them lightly with a fork). Microwave on high for thirty seconds. Remove from the microwave and stir, then cook on high for another fifteen seconds, and they should be fully cooked.

COUSCOUS: Place a one-to-one ratio of couscous and water in a microwave-safe bowl. Place a microwave-safe dish on top of the bowl and microwave on high for five minutes. Remove the bowl from the microwave, fluff the couscous with a fork, cover again with the plate, and let the couscous sit for five minutes, by which point it should have absorbed all the water.

PASTA: This method works for all kinds of packaged dried pasta, including protein/chickpea-based and whole wheat. To achieve al dente pasta, place a one-to-three ratio of pasta to water with a pinch of salt in a microwave-safe bowl and microwave uncovered on high for five minutes. Remove the bowl from the microwave and stir the pasta. Return to the microwave and microwave on high for another five minutes, then drain.

RICE NOODLES: Place a one-to-three ratio of rice noodles and water in a microwave-safe bowl. Cover with a microwave-safe plate and microwave on high for five to six minutes. Remove from the microwave and let sit, covered, for one minute before draining.

REHEATING FOOD: Basically all foods in this book can be reheated in a microwave, although previously baked or breaded foods often retain their proper texture better when reheated in an air fryer or toaster oven. Place the food in the microwave and microwave on high for thirty seconds to one minute. Food does not need to be covered when microwaving, although you can place a paper towel over the top to catch splatters.

RICE COOKER

Yes, rice cookers are designed to cook rice to perfection. But they can do a lot more! With some models, you can basically cook any meal that requires a hot plate or stovetop and a frying pan. For example, you can fry cubed chicken in a rice cooker in about ten minutes and even cook soups within half an hour. The typical rice cooker reaches a temperature that is comparable to medium-high heat on the stovetop.

None of the recipes in this book calls for a rice cooker, but you are welcome to try using one if you like. Refer to the user manual for your particular model for cooking instructions.

SLOW COOKER

A slow cooker is great for making stews, soups, and dips. I use a medium-sized 4½-quart slow cooker. I recommend this size because the recipes in this book are for one to four servings. Your slow cooker doesn't need to be fancy or have any special buttons. As long as it has both low and high cook settings, you are set.

You don't need a slow cooker with a nonstick interior. If you want to make cleanup easier, you can use plastic slow cooker liners, which you can buy at grocery stores.

COOKING TIPS

When I have leftovers from a slow cooker meal, I don't take the time and energy to place the extra food in a separate container before refrigerating it. Instead, I let it cool completely, then remove the pot from the base, cover it with its lid, and place the whole thing in the refrigerator. When it's time to reheat those leftovers, I just place the pot back into the base and turn the slow cooker to low. Reheating usually takes about twenty minutes.

Sometimes, I prepare the ingredients and assemble the slow cooker meal in the evening so that it cooks throughout the night while I am sleeping. Then I wake up to a meal that's ready for lunch or dinner later that day.

TOASTER OVEN

Baking in a toaster oven is just as good as baking in a full-sized oven. A toaster oven heats up a lot faster, too! For the greatest flexibility, in almost all of the recipes that use an oven, I give the choice of using either a toaster oven or a conventional oven. (The exceptions are the recipes that are too large to fit in a toaster oven.)

The primary difference between the two types of ovens is that some dishes take longer to cook in the toaster oven. Therefore, the cooking time is given in a range to reflect this difference. If using a conventional oven, be sure to check the dish at the low end of the cooking time range; if using a toaster oven, the dish will likely be done at the higher end of the range of time. As always, go by the description of when the dish is done.

I recommend a medium-sized toaster oven that comes with one or more baking trays and a removable crumb tray. (A larger toaster oven works if you have the counter space for it.) I also recommend having a timer feature that shuts off the oven at the end of the cook time. I find it useful to have a broiler function, too.

COOKING TIPS

A toaster oven is a great tool for reheating leftovers. Preheat the toaster oven to 375°F and bake the food for about five minutes.

HOT PLATE

It's amazing what you can cook using a hot plate. Some hot plates come with one burner and others come with two, which gives you more options. If you don't have a stove but want to do stovetop-type cooking, a hot plate is indispensable.

I suggest a hot plate with a wattage of 1,000 to 1,800. (Most models fall within that range.) I use the Elite Gourmet Countertop Single Cast Iron Burner with the temperature control knob; it's an excellent and affordable cooking tool. The knob enables you to easily adjust the heat settings while cooking.

It is best to preheat the hot plate before using it, which takes about five minutes. After using the hot plate, make sure to let it cool to room temperature before cleaning and storing it.

KITCHENWARE AND TOOLS

To prepare the recipes in this book, you will need some essential pieces of kitchenware and tools. Having these items will make the preparing, cooking, and cleaning process easier and less time-consuming.

- **Aluminum foil or parchment paper:** I use either foil or parchment to line pans for easy cleanup. When using parchment paper for air-frying, make sure it is fitted to the air-fryer basket. Never run the fryer without having food on top of the parchment. Unweighted parchment paper might fly around and touch the heating element, which is a fire hazard.

- **Baking dishes:** I prefer ceramic baking dishes in 1-, 2-, and 3-quart sizes, but oven-safe glass dishes also work.

- **Baking pans:** The recipes in this book call for a 9-inch square baking pan and a 13 by 9-inch baking pan.

- **Chef's knife:** I recommend finding a chef's knife that fits comfortably in your hand. It's best not to wash the knife in the dishwasher (if you even have one in your compact kitchen) because the knife can be damaged in the dishwasher. I find stainless steel knives are the best. I also recommend having a knife sharpener so you can keep the knife well sharpened.

- **Food processor, mini:** If you'd like to make the Date Caramel Dip (page 218), you'll need a mini food processor. A 3- to 4-cup model will do the job. You can also use a mini food processor to turn rolled oats into oat flour for my Cake for Breakfast recipe on page 60.

- **Frying pans:** Small (8-inch), medium-sized (10-inch), and large (12-inch). Nonstick frying pans make cleanup easier, but if you do not have nonstick pans, then greased regular frying pans work just as well.

- **Instant-read thermometer:** To check the internal temperature of cooked meats as well as the heat-treated flour in my Strawberries & Cream Cookie Dough (page 138).

- **Measuring cups (liquid and dry) and spoons:** Get a set of dry measuring cups for measuring all things dry or nonliquid—oats, rice, shredded carrots—and to level off the top with a knife for exact quantities of flour. Clear glass or plastic spouted measuring cups are what you need for measuring liquids; 1-cup and 2-cup are the most practical sizes.

- **Microwave-safe bowls and plates:** Bowls that have a diameter of 3 to 6 inches or 7 to 10 inches and round dinner plates that are 6 to 10 inches in diameter work best.

- **Mixing bowls:** In various sizes.

- **Muffin pans:** I use a standard-sized twelve-well muffin pan for the Any Berry French Toast Muffins (page 58) and a mini muffin pan for the Raspberry-Filled Frozen Yogurt Bites (page 222). You can also buy smaller muffin pans designed for use in a toaster oven.

- **Paper muffin cup liners:** Standard-sized and mini.

- **Pie dish, mini:** I use a 6-inch deep pie dish with 2-inch-high sides for Polenta Pie (page 148). If you don't have a mini pie dish, you can use a 1-quart baking dish instead.

- **Saucepan:** A 2-quart saucepan will serve you well for all the recipes in this book. I use mine for simple tasks like boiling potatoes and for making super easy stovetop soups and one-pot pasta dishes.

- **Sheet pans:** When using a toaster oven, you will need a small sheet pan such as a quarter sheet pan, which measures 13 by 9 inches. If your toaster oven is too small to accommodate a quarter sheet pan, then you will need a 10 by 7-inch sheet pan. If you are using a full-sized oven, then a standard-sized 18 by 13-inch half sheet pan will work fine.

SHOPPING LIST

For convenience, the recipes in this book use a limited number of ingredients so that you can use up the food you buy before it spoils. The idea is to stock your refrigerator, freezer, and pantry with key items and then use those same items to make a variety of yummy meals. For example, eggs are a common ingredient in the savory breakfast section. Another example is sausage, which is used in the Roasted Veggie & Sausage Sheet Pan Breakfast (page 44) and the Everything but the Kitchen Sink Soup (page 82).

MEAT AND SEAFOOD

- **Beef:** I don't use a lot of beef in my cooking, but in this book there are two recipes that call for boneless beef chuck roast and one that calls for lean ground beef.

- **Chicken:** For the recipes in this book, I use either boneless, skinless chicken breast or shredded cooked chicken breast. (For the latter, a store-bought rotisserie chicken will save you time and effort.) If you prefer dark meat, swap in boneless, skinless chicken thighs.

- **Fish:** Recipes in this book call for cod, salmon, and tilapia fillets and imitation crab meat, which is made with fish.

- **Ham:** Preferably sliced deli ham.

- **Pepperoni:** Either turkey-based or pork and beef–based pepperoni works well in these recipes.

- **Sausage:** Turkey, pork, chicken, or beef. I like to use fully cooked breakfast sausage links and smoked sausage (such as Hillshire Farm).

- **Shrimp:** Shrimp is a great compact cooking ingredient because you can keep it in the freezer and pull out as many as you need when you're in the mood for shrimp. In this book, I use medium shrimp (fresh or frozen) and small shrimp (frozen, precooked).

- **Turkey:** I often use ground turkey in recipes where ground beef is traditional (like in my Hearty Turkey Chili on page 188), and sliced deli turkey is practically a staple in my fridge for easy sandwiches. For the Turkey Salad Sandwich with Dried Cherries (page 114), a post–Thanksgiving Day invention and a delicious change from the more typical chicken salad, I use shredded cooked turkey, although rotisserie chicken can be substituted.

- Turkey bacon

DAIRY, EGGS, AND TOFU

- **Butter:** Any kind of butter works for these recipes, whether it is dairy or plant-based. If you opt for salted butter rather than unsalted, make sure to use less salt than the recipe calls for.

- **Cheeses:** I use a variety of cheeses in my recipes, ranging from soft and semi-hard to hard (such as Brie, cheddar, and Parmesan), and in various forms (crumbled, shredded, grated, and sliced). In most cases, I specify the type that I think works for that dish; however, feel free to substitute other cheeses of the same basic type (soft, semi-hard, or hard) according to what you have on hand or prefer. Note that traditional Parmesan cheese is made with animal rennet, making it unsuitable for vegetarians; if you are a vegetarian, buy Parmesan cheese labeled "no animal rennet" or something similar.

- **Cream cheese:** Except for recipes that require whipped cream cheese, like my Chocolate Protein Cheesecake Dip (page 214), I use cream cheese with one-third less fat (aka Neufchâtel cheese when in block form) due to the lower fat and calorie content. However, full-fat cream cheese works as well.

- **Eggs:** I use large grade A chicken eggs for the recipes in this book.

- **Greek yogurt, plain and vanilla-flavored:** I use plain Greek yogurt in savory recipes (such as Chicken Tikka Masala on page 194) and vanilla-flavored yogurt for recipes with a sweet flavor profile. With the exception of the Cookies & Cream Frozen Yogurt recipe (page 206), which requires full-fat Greek yogurt for the best texture, you can use a full-fat yogurt for extra creaminess or a reduced-fat or even nonfat yogurt for fewer calories and a leaner form of protein.

- **Half-and-half:** I love the flexibility of half-and-half. It's just rich enough to add a touch of creaminess to any recipe, and you can use it in your morning coffee. Plus, it keeps longer than milk. Unsweetened canned coconut cream is a good dairy-free substitute for half-and-half.

- **Milk:** Use any milk you prefer, whether it is skim, 2%, whole milk, or a plant-based milk such as nut or oat milk. When using plant-based milk in savory recipes, be sure to use unflavored and unsweetened milk.

- **Tofu, firm:** I use firm tofu to make meat-free cabbage rolls (see page 162). You can store block-form tofu in the refrigerator for two weeks and in the freezer for two months.

BREADS, PASTA, AND GRAINS

- **Breads:** I choose whole wheat sandwich bread and flatbread for added nutrients and fiber. If you're gluten-intolerant, feel free to substitute gluten-free bread.

- **Couscous:** Often assumed to be a grain due to its appearance, couscous is actually a type of pasta made of semolina (granules of durum wheat). It is traditionally used in North African dishes, such as tagine, but I use it anytime I need a starchy side to accompany a dish, and particularly when I am pressed for time. (It takes all of five minutes to prepare.)

- **Oats:** All of the recipes in this book, save one, call for rolled oats; for the Microwave Cranberry Pecan Breakfast Cookie on page 70, you'll need quick oats.

- **Pasta and noodles:** I use a variety of pasta shapes, from bowtie to rigatoni and everything in between (and of course macaroni for mac and cheese; see my recipe on page 150). For the best nutritional value, I recommend high-protein pasta and whole wheat pasta; however, regular pasta will work with these recipes. For Faux Pho (page 78), my easy take on the classic Vietnamese soup, and Spicy Dumpling Noodle Soup (page 80), you'll need vermicelli rice noodles.

- **Polenta, uncooked:** Polenta is a key ingredient in one of my family's favorite dishes, my mom's savory Polenta Pie (page 148). For this recipe, you want the kind that comes in a bag or box, not the cooked kind that is sold in tubes. Store uncooked polenta in an airtight container in a cool, dry, and dark place, such as a pantry, away from anything that gives off heat.

- **Pretzels:** I typically use whole wheat pretzels for added nutrients and fiber, but regular pretzels are fine, too. For the recipes in this book, you'll need mini-twist pretzels.

- **Rice:** Either white or brown rice works well in these recipes.

- **Tortillas, 5-inch corn and 10-inch flour:** I choose whole wheat flour tortillas for added nutrients and fiber. Gluten-free flour tortillas can be substituted throughout. Corn tortillas are naturally gluten-free.

OILS

- **Coconut oil, refined:** Due to its neutral flavor, I use refined coconut oil rather than virgin. You'll need some for the Baked Spiced Peach (page 52) and the Handy-Dandy Candy Bars (page 236). (Another benefit to refined over virgin coconut oil is its high smoke point; try using it the next time you want to fry something over high heat.)

- **Cooking oil spray:** I prefer olive oil spray, but any type will work. In addition to greasing pans, I like to spray it on both sides of a sandwich before cooking the sandwich in my air fryer.

- **Olive oil:** Use extra-virgin olive oil when making salad dressings and pure olive oil for cooking.

- **Toasted sesame oil:** The nutty flavor of toasted sesame oil adds great flavor to dishes. Look for pure sesame oil, with no other ingredients. I tend to use this in my noodle bowl recipes in the lunch section to add some extra flavor and healthy fats.

- **Vegetable oil:** I tend to use vegetable oil in baking. You'll use it for my breakfast cookie and mug cake (on pages 70 and 234, respectively).

FRUITS

In the recipes, any of the fruits listed below will work, and you can use fresh, frozen, or canned. It's best to defrost frozen fruit before use unless the recipe states otherwise. If using canned fruit, make sure to drain and discard the juice (or set it aside for another use).

- Apples
- Bananas
- Blueberries
- Cherries
- Grapefruit
- Kiwi
- Lemons
- Mango
- Peaches
- Raspberries
- Strawberries

VEGETABLES

As with fruit, fresh, frozen, or canned vegetables will work for these recipes. Thaw frozen vegetables before using them unless the recipe states otherwise. If you are using canned vegetables, drain and discard or reserve the canning liquid.

Some of the foods listed below are technically botanical fruits. However, they still offer the same nutritional values as vegetables, being lesser in sugar and having a more savory flavor.

- Avocados
- Bell peppers: All colors
- Broccoli
- Cabbage: Green
- Carrots
- Celery
- Cucumbers
- Garlic
- Green beans
- Green onions (aka scallions)
- Mushrooms: Button and portabella
- Onions: Yellow and red
- Potatoes: You will need sweet potatoes and russets, along with baby and regular-sized reds and all-purpose potatoes like Yukon Golds or Red Golds.
- Spinach
- Spring mix
- Squash: Butternut, spaghetti, yellow summer squash, and zucchini
- Sugar snap peas
- Tomatoes

SAUCES AND CONDIMENTS

- **Dressings:** I usually make my own salad dressings. A handful of the recipes call for prepared ranch and Italian dressing, but you can always make them from scratch if you prefer.

- **Hot sauce and wing sauce:** Small jars with big flavor! Perfect for compact cooking. For hot sauces, my go-tos are Sriracha sauce and a medium-hot hot sauce such as Frank's RedHot Original Cayenne Pepper Sauce. I also use Buffalo wing sauce in my Buffalo Chicken Salad Sandwich (page 108) and Microwave Buffalo Chicken Mac & Cheese (page 150). But of course you can always use Buffalo sauce to make wings.

- **Lemon juice:** Fresh and pre-squeezed lemon juice are both great options.

- **Marinara sauce:** Any marinara sauce works for the recipes that call for it. However, marinara sauce without added sugar is the best.

- **Mayonnaise:** I prefer olive oil–based mayonnaise, but the regular kind works perfectly, too. Buy vegan mayo if you need to avoid eggs.

- **Pesto:** I love Classico brand pesto because you can find it in most any grocery store, and it pairs perfectly with any egg dish. Leftover jarred pesto keeps well, lasting about three weeks in the refrigerator.

- **Soy sauce:** An indispensable seasoning for giving authentic Asian flair and umami to a number of dishes. It is quite salty, so always taste the final dish before adding more sauce or salt to taste. Note that regular soy sauce contains gluten, but if you are gluten-free, you can purchase gluten-free soy sauce or tamari instead.

- **Tomato paste:** This is the secret ingredient in a killer pot roast and the not-so-secret ingredient in a great pasta dish. Once opened, a can of tomato paste will keep for five to seven days in the fridge, or up to three months in the freezer. To freeze it, simply remove the paste from the can, portion it into tablespoon quantities onto a small lined tray, freeze until solid, and then pop into a freezer bag.

- **Tomato sauce:** Any tomato sauce works perfectly with the recipes that call for it. However, sauces that are purely tomatoes and salt work the best.

- **Vinegars:** For the recipes in this book, you'll need red wine vinegar and unseasoned rice vinegar; if you enjoy making your own salad dressings, I suggest keeping a bottle of white wine vinegar and balsamic vinegar in your pantry as well.

BAKING INGREDIENTS AND SWEETENERS

- All-purpose flour

- Applesauce, unsweetened: Applesauce is a great way to add moisture and sweetness to baked goods while reducing the use of refined sugar and/or oil. I use it in my Microwave Cranberry Pecan Breakfast Cookie (page 70).

- Baking powder

- Cocoa powder

- Dark chocolate chips and bars: 60 to 70 percent cacao is optimal.

- Dried fruit: Cherries and cranberries (both sweetened)

- Freeze-dried strawberries: I sometimes use these as an alternative to fresh strawberries in my Strawberries & Cream Cookie Dough (page 238).

- Gluten-free flours: I use oat flour in the Cake for Breakfast recipe on page 60, although if you have a blender, you can use ground rolled oats in place of oat flour. Finely ground blanched almond flour is my flour of choice for the Protein Brownie Balls (page 54); it gives them a wonderfully soft yet chewy texture and ups the protein content. But you can use oat flour in its place if you prefer.

  Nut flours and whole grain flours, such as oat flour, are more perishable than all-purpose flour. To prolong the freshness of almond flour, store it in the refrigerator, where it will keep for six months, or in the freezer, where it will keep for a year. Oat flour should be stored in a cool, dark place and will generally keep for a few months.

- Nuts: I typically buy sliced almonds, pecans, pine nuts, pistachios, walnuts, and roasted mixed nuts. Many of the recipes in this book were developed with a specific type of nut in mind; for others, you can use any nut you like. That said, for even those recipes that call for a specific nut, if you don't have that type on hand, you can substitute whatever kind you think would work well in its place.

- Sweeteners: I like granulated monk fruit sweetener because it is sugar-free and has a similar texture and sweetness level to granulated sugar. I also use honey (I buy pure clover honey in a squeezable bottle) and maple syrup, which are natural sweeteners that also have some nutrients, along with small amounts of granulated sugar and brown sugar. If you would like to swap in a different type of sweetener for the type called for in a recipe, here are the equivalents:

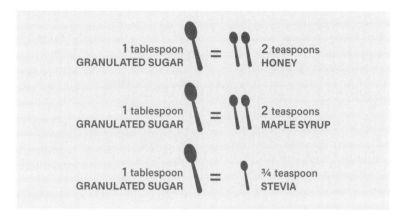

1 tablespoon GRANULATED SUGAR	=	2 teaspoons HONEY
1 tablespoon GRANULATED SUGAR	=	2 teaspoons MAPLE SYRUP
1 tablespoon GRANULATED SUGAR	=	¾ teaspoon STEVIA

- Vanilla extract
- White chocolate chips and bars

SPICES AND SEASONINGS

- Crushed red pepper
- Dried chives
- Dried dill weed
- Dried minced onions
- Dried parsley
- Garlic powder
- Garlic salt
- Ginger powder
- Ground black pepper
- Ground cinnamon
- Ground dried oregano
- Ground dried thyme
- Italian seasoning
- Onion powder
- Paprika, both smoked and regular (aka sweet)
- Pumpkin pie spice
- Iodized table salt
- Turmeric powder

FROZEN FOODS

- Berries, mixed
- Blueberries
- Broccoli florets
- Dumplings: Veggie, chicken, or pork
- Peppers and onions medley
- Raspberries
- Shrimp, small precooked: See the Meat and Seafood list on page 16 for more on this handy frozen protein.
- Vegetables, mixed

OTHER CANNED, JARRED, OR BOXED FOODS

- Bacon bits: I buy McCormick brand. You could also crumble some cooked bacon or turkey bacon and use it wherever bacon bits are called for in this book.
- Beans and lentils: The recipes in this book use canned chickpeas, black beans, and cannellini beans.
- Bouillon: I sometimes use chicken bouillon cubes when I want to make a recipe extra portable, like my Faux Pho (page 78).
- Broth: I mostly use chicken broth in the recipes, though sometimes I opt for vegetable or beef broth. However, any variety can be used, depending on what you have on hand or prefer to use. If you are watching your sodium intake, use a low-sodium broth.
- Coconut cream: Unsweetened canned coconut cream is a great dairy-free swap for half-and-half in the recipes in this book.
- Jam: I tend to use fig, raspberry, and strawberry jams, preferably ones that are low in sugar (but regular is fine if that's what you like).
- Peanut butter: Use natural peanut butter without added salt or sweetener. For most of the recipes, either chunky or creamy can be used, according to your preference. When a certain texture is better for a recipe, I've noted that in the ingredient list.
- Protein powder: I like to add vanilla- or chocolate-flavored protein powder to sweet recipes.
- Sliced black olives

chapter 1:

SIMPLE BREAKFASTS

Crunched for time to make breakfast? Still sleepy but also hungry? No problem! All the recipes in this chapter are super easy to make. Some are quick, and others require minimal effort.

I don't know about you, but one morning I'll crave something savory for breakfast, and the next day I'll crave something sweet. If you can relate, then you will be happy to know that this chapter is divided into two parts: "Feelin' Somethin' Savory?" and "Feelin' Somethin' Sweet?" Each section has a variety of recipes to satisfy your cravings, provide exceptional nutrition, and keep you full for hours. I hope you enjoy them as much as I do!

FEELIN' SOMETHIN' SAVORY?

FEELIN' SOMETHIN' SWEET?

LAZY TOMATO & EGG BAKE

OPTION

YIELD: 1 serving   **PREP TIME:** 10 minutes   **COOK TIME:** 32 to 55 minutes

This is one of my mother's favorite recipes to make for breakfast, lunch, or dinner. In my opinion, this dish feels like a warm hug on a sunny morning. It is so easy to put together and cook to your liking. I prefer runny egg yolks, but my mom likes hers cooked through. I will let you decide which way is better!

2 cups grape tomatoes

2 tablespoons olive oil

1 tablespoon minced garlic

1 tablespoon chopped fresh parsley

½ teaspoon crushed red pepper

Pinch of salt

Pinch of ground black pepper

2 large eggs

¼ cup shredded semi-hard cheese of choice

Sliced green onions, for garnish (optional)

2 slices whole wheat bread, toasted, for serving

1. Preheat the toaster oven or oven to 350°F.

2. Dump the tomatoes, olive oil, garlic, parsley, crushed red pepper, salt, and black pepper into a 2-quart baking dish. Bake for 20 to 25 minutes, until the tomatoes have begun to burst and shrivel.

3. Take the dish out of the oven and crush the tomatoes slightly, then make two wells in the mixture and crack an egg into each well.

4. Return the dish to the oven and bake for another 10 to 13 minutes for runny yolks or 20 to 23 minutes for fully cooked yolks.

5. Top with the cheese and bake for 2 minutes more, or until the cheese has melted. Garnish with sliced green onions, if desired, and enjoy with toast. Best served fresh but can last in the fridge for up to 4 days. To reheat, microwave on medium-high for 1 minute.

ALLERGENS

NOTE: To make this dish gluten-free, use gluten-free bread or omit the toast altogether.

PEPPER & EGGS

OPTION

YIELD: 1 serving   **PREP TIME:** 5 minutes
COOK TIME: 6 to 23 minutes, depending on method

This no-fuss recipe is one of the easiest in this book. I love to use this dish as a tasty filling for a breakfast sandwich while traveling or when I need extra energy in the morning. Sometimes I find myself making it for dinner too because of how hearty it is and how effortlessly it comes together. If you don't have an air fryer, you can use the oven or toaster oven.

1 small to medium red bell pepper

2 large eggs

Pinch of salt

Pinch of ground black pepper

Pinch of crushed red pepper

2 slices whole wheat bread, toasted, for serving (optional)

Sliced green onions, for garnish (optional)

1. *If using an air fryer,* line the air-fryer basket with aluminum foil or parchment paper.

If using the toaster oven or oven, preheat it to 350°F.

2. Lay the bell pepper on its side and, working from the center outward, cut two 1-inch rings. Remove the seeds and membranes, then place the rings in the prepared air-fryer basket or, if using the oven, in a small baking dish. (Save the rest of the bell pepper for another recipe.)

3. Crack an egg into the center of each bell pepper ring and season with the salt, black pepper, and crushed red pepper.

4. *If using an air fryer,* air-fry at 375°F for 6 to 7 minutes for firm whites and runny yolks or up to 10 minutes if you prefer fully cooked yolks.

If using the oven, bake for 10 to 13 minutes for firm whites and runny yolks or 20 to 23 minutes for fully cooked yolks.

5. Serve on toast, if desired, garnished with sliced green onions.

ALLERGENS

NOTE: To make this dish gluten-free, use gluten-free bread or omit the toast altogether.

BREAKFAST QUESADILLA

OPTION

YIELD: 1 serving   **PREP TIME:** 5 minutes
COOK TIME: 6 to 12 minutes, depending on method

This quesadilla was a favorite breakfast of mine while I was completing my dietetic internship. It takes minimal effort and is perfect for meal prep. Just cook it the night before and stash it in the fridge. The next morning, heat it up in the microwave and enjoy it on the go! I prefer to use the air fryer for efficiency here—no need to preheat a frying pan.

2 large eggs

1 tablespoon milk of choice

¼ cup shredded part-skim mozzarella cheese

2 (10-inch) whole wheat flour tortillas

2 teaspoons medium-hot hot sauce, such as Frank's RedHot Original

Pinch of onion powder

Pinch of salt

Pinch of ground black pepper

Sliced green onions, for garnish (optional)

NOTE: To make this quesadilla gluten-free, use gluten-free tortillas.

1. In a small bowl, beat the eggs and milk together. Scramble the egg mixture either on the stovetop or, if you're pressed for time, in the microwave.

To scramble the eggs on the stovetop, pour the egg mixture into a medium-sized greased frying pan set over medium-high heat and scramble with a rubber spatula until done, 3 to 4 minutes.

To scramble the eggs in the microwave, pour the egg mixture into a medium-sized microwave-safe bowl and microwave on medium-high for 45 seconds. Take out and stir, then microwave again for 45 seconds, or until done.

2. Place the scrambled eggs and cheese on top of one of the tortillas and season with the hot sauce, onion powder, salt, and pepper. Top with the second tortilla.

3. *To cook the quesadilla in an air fryer,* place it in the air-fryer basket and air-fry at 375°F for 5 minutes, or until the top turns a light golden brown, then flip it over and air-fry for another 3 minutes, or until the quesadilla is golden brown on both sides and the cheese has melted.

To cook the quesadilla on the stovetop, coat a large frying pan with cooking oil spray and set it over medium-high heat. Once the pan is hot, place the quesadilla in the pan and cook until the bottom tortilla is lightly golden brown, about 3 minutes. Flip the quesadilla over and continue cooking until the other side is golden brown and the cheese has melted, another 3 minutes or so.

4. To serve, cut into four slices. Garnish with sliced green onions, if desired.

ALLERGENS

SAVORY EGG CUPS

  YIELD: 1 or 2 servings **PREP TIME:** 8 minutes
COOK TIME: 7 to 23 minutes, depending on method

When I wake up in the mood for something savory, I sometimes make these easy egg cups. I love this recipe because it is super quick and nearly effortless. If I want a lighter breakfast, I'll eat just one egg cup; two cups are perfect when I need a breakfast with real staying power. These egg cups are perfect for enjoying on the go and can be refrigerated for up to a week or frozen for up to two months. Serve them with a slice of toast, if desired.

½ cup chopped tomatoes

¼ cup chopped red onions

2 large eggs

¼ cup shredded cheddar cheese

Pinch of garlic powder

Pinch of onion powder

Pinch of salt

Pinch of ground black pepper

Snipped fresh chives or chopped fresh herb of choice, for garnish (optional)

1. *If using the toaster oven or oven,* preheat it to 350°F.

2. Grease two 4-ounce ramekins or oven-safe bowls with cooking oil spray, then evenly divide the tomatoes and onions between them. Crack an egg into each ramekin or bowl. Top with the cheese, then season with the garlic powder, onion powder, salt, and pepper.

3. *If using an air fryer,* air-fry at 360°F for 7 to 10 minutes, depending on how you like your eggs: 7 minutes will create runnier yolks, and 10 minutes will give you more fully cooked yolks.

If using the oven, bake for 10 to 13 minutes for runny yolks or 20 to 23 minutes for fully cooked yolks.

4. Take out the egg cups and garnish with chives, if desired.

ALLERGENS

BREAKFAST FRIES

 YIELD: 1 serving   **PREP TIME:** 10 minutes, plus 20 minutes to soak potatoes
COOK TIME: 14 to 30 minutes, depending on method

My father created this recipe one Saturday after asking me what I wanted for breakfast. I told him french fries, so he made me these breakfast fries, and they've been a family favorite ever since. You can eat them with ketchup or hot sauce (I prefer hot sauce). If using an air fryer, this recipe takes only about 25 minutes to prep and cook and is perfect for when you are craving something savory in the morning! You can add an egg for extra protein, but the fries are great as they are.

1 medium russet potato, scrubbed

1 large egg (optional)

1 tablespoon olive oil, plus 1 teaspoon for the egg (if using)

½ teaspoon onion powder

½ teaspoon paprika

¼ teaspoon garlic powder

Pinch of salt

Pinch of ground black pepper

⅓ cup shredded semi-hard cheese of choice

FOR TOPPING/SERVING

2 tablespoons bacon bits

½ cup diced tomatoes

Sliced green onions

Ketchup or hot sauce

1. *If using the toaster oven or oven,* preheat it to 400°F. Line a small sheet pan with parchment paper.

2. Slice the potato into ¼-inch-wide strips that resemble french fries. Soak the strips in a bowl of ice-cold water for 20 minutes.

3. If using the egg, scramble it with 1 teaspoon of olive oil in a small greased frying pan over medium heat until soft curds form, about 5 minutes. Remove from the pan and set aside.

4. Drain the potato strips and pat dry. Season the strips with the olive oil, onion powder, paprika, garlic powder, salt, and pepper.

5. *If using an air fryer,* place the potato strips in the air-fryer basket and air-fry at 380°F for 12 minutes, or until crispy.

If using the oven, place the fries on the prepared pan and bake for 20 to 23 minutes, until crispy. Halfway through baking, flip the fries over so they brown evenly on both sides.

6. Sprinkle the cheese and the scrambled egg, if using, on top of the fries and air-fry or bake for 2 minutes more, or until the cheese has melted.

7. Top the fries with the bacon bits and tomatoes. Garnish with green onions and enjoy with ketchup or hot sauce.

ALLERGENS

OPTION

NOTE: To make these fries egg-free, omit the scrambled egg.

EGG IN A BASKET

OPTION

YIELD: 1 serving   **PREP TIME:** 5 minutes
COOK TIME: 2½ to 13 minutes, depending on method

You've probably eaten or at least heard of the dish known as eggs in a basket, sometimes called eggs in a hole or eggs in a nest. This was one of the first recipes I ever made as a kid, and I loved it so much that I continued to make it into adulthood. Using an air fryer makes this version even quicker and easier, with less cleanup. If you don't have an air fryer, you can make it in a frying pan on the stovetop or even on a hot plate.

1 slice whole wheat bread

1 large egg

Pinch of salt

Pinch of ground black pepper

Pinch of garlic powder

Pinch of onion powder

Pinch of crushed red pepper

¼ cup shredded part-skim mozzarella cheese

Sliced green onions, for garnish (optional)

1. *If using an air fryer,* line the air-fryer basket with parchment paper.

2. Lightly coat both sides of the bread with cooking oil spray, then cut a 2- to 2½-inch hole in the center of the bread.

3. Place the bread (both the slice and the round cutout) in the prepared air-fryer basket or in a medium-sized greased frying pan.

4. Crack the egg into the hole in the center of the bread. Season the egg with the salt, pepper, garlic powder, onion powder, and crushed red pepper.

5. *If using an air fryer,* air-fry at 340°F for 4 to 5 minutes. Top with the cheese and air-fry for 4 to 5 minutes more for a solid white and semi-solid yolk. If you desire a fully cooked yolk, air-fry for an additional 3 minutes.

If using a hot plate or the stovetop, cook over medium heat for 2 to 3 minutes, depending how runny you like the yolk, then flip and top with the cheese. Cover with a lid and cook until the cheese has melted, another 30 seconds or so.

6. Garnish with sliced green onions, if desired, and serve.

ALLERGENS

NOTE: To make this dish gluten-free, use gluten-free bread.

CAPRESE TOAST

OPTION

YIELD: 1 serving **PREP TIME:** 5 minutes
COOK TIME: 3 to 8 minutes, depending on method

Caprese anything has been a favorite of mine ever since Panera Bread came out with its caprese panini. I mean, what's not to love about it? There is creamy mozzarella cheese and fresh tomatoes, and the combination of basil, garlic, and olive oil is a dream. I love that sandwich so much that I created this quick on-the-go breakfast version, ideally cooked in a toaster oven. Hopefully you'll love it too!

1 small Roma tomato, sliced

2 thick slices part-skim mozzarella cheese, diced

1 slice whole wheat bread, toasted

1 tablespoon olive oil

¼ teaspoon dried basil

Pinch of salt

Pinch of ground black pepper

Pinch of garlic powder

1. *If using the toaster oven or oven,* preheat it to 400°F.

2. Lay the tomato slices and mozzarella on the toast. Place in the air-fryer basket or, if using the oven, on a small sheet pan.

3. Air-fry at 375°F for 3 to 5 minutes or bake in the oven for 5 to 8 minutes, until the cheese is slightly melted.

4. Drizzle with the olive oil and top with a sprinkling of dried basil. Season with the salt, pepper, and garlic powder and enjoy!

ALLERGENS

NOTE: To make this toast gluten-free, use gluten-free bread.

BREAKFAST BAKE

OPTION

YIELD: 2 servings   **PREP TIME:** 10 minutes   **COOK TIME:** 20 minutes

Imagine this: you wake up one Sunday morning and you want a nice, warming breakfast for two. But because it's the weekend, you want to keep it simple. Therefore, you make this easy, savory bake, which hits the spot. Before you know it, you will be making it every Sunday morning! Enjoy it with toast or on its own.

5 large eggs

3 slices turkey bacon

½ cup chopped yellow onions

½ cup chopped bell peppers (any color)

4 ounces fully cooked breakfast sausage links, sliced

½ cup shredded cheddar or part-skim mozzarella cheese

½ teaspoon garlic powder

½ teaspoon crushed red pepper

Snipped fresh chives or chopped fresh herb of choice, for garnish (optional)

2 slices whole wheat bread, toasted, for serving (optional)

1. Preheat the toaster oven or oven to 375°F. Grease a 2-quart baking dish.

2. In a medium-sized mixing bowl, whisk the eggs until the whites and yolks are fully combined.

3. Slice the bacon crosswise into ½-inch pieces and add them to the eggs.

4. To the same bowl, add the onions, bell peppers, sausage, cheese, garlic powder, and crushed red pepper and stir to combine.

5. Pour the mixture into the prepared baking dish and bake for 15 to 20 minutes, until the eggs are cooked through and set.

6. Garnish with chives, if desired, and enjoy on its own or with toast. Best served fresh but can be refrigerated for up to 4 days or frozen for up to 2 months. To reheat, microwave on medium-high for 1 to 2 minutes.

ALLERGENS

NOTE: To make this dish gluten-free, use gluten-free bread or omit the toast altogether.

ROASTED VEGGIE & SAUSAGE SHEET PAN BREAKFAST

OPTION

YIELD: 3 servings   **PREP TIME:** 10 minutes   **COOK TIME:** 20 minutes

Nothing beats a warm sheet pan breakfast that takes only ten minutes to prepare. For this recipe, all you need to do is chop and season the vegetables and throw it all on a sheet pan—the oven takes care of the rest. The sausage adds a tasty high-quality protein, and the fact that it's precooked makes life so much easier. This breakfast is perfect to enjoy with others too!

1 cup frozen broccoli florets

1 cup sliced bell peppers (any color)

1 cup sliced yellow summer squash

3 tablespoons olive oil

½ teaspoon salt

½ teaspoon ground black pepper

½ teaspoon garlic powder

½ teaspoon onion powder

½ teaspoon Italian seasoning

4 ounces fully cooked breakfast sausage links, sliced

3 slices whole wheat bread, toasted, for serving (optional)

1. Preheat the toaster oven or oven to 400°F. Line a small sheet pan with parchment paper or aluminum foil.

2. Place the broccoli, bell peppers, and squash on the prepared pan. Season with the olive oil, salt, pepper, garlic powder, onion powder, and Italian seasoning and toss to evenly coat. Arrange the sausage slices in the center of the pan.

3. Roast for 15 to 20 minutes, or until the vegetables are fork-tender and lightly browned. Enjoy with toast, if desired.

4. Store leftovers in the fridge for up to 4 days, or freeze for up to a month. To reheat, microwave on medium-high for 1 minute 30 seconds.

NOTE: To make this dish gluten-free, use gluten-free bread or omit the toast altogether.

OMELETS ON TOAST

YIELD: 2 servings **PREP TIME:** 10 minutes
COOK TIME: 7 to 21 minutes, depending on method

This recipe is a lifesaver, especially when you are craving something warm, savory, and filling in the morning. It has an ideal ratio of carbs, fats, and protein, and the onions and peppers make it the perfect nutritious and balanced meal. It is also handy for when you're in a rush! I like to make it in my air fryer, but if you don't have one, you can use the oven.

2 large eggs

¼ cup diced red onions

¼ cup diced bell peppers (any color)

Pinch of salt

Pinch of ground black pepper

Pinch of garlic powder

2 slices whole wheat bread

½ cup shredded part-skim mozzarella cheese

Sliced green onions, for garnish (optional)

1. *If using the toaster oven or oven,* preheat it to 375°F and line a small sheet pan with parchment paper.

If using an air fryer, line the air-fryer basket with parchment paper.

2. In a medium-sized bowl, beat the eggs well, then add the onions, bell peppers, salt, pepper, and garlic powder and whisk to combine.

3. Press down on the center of each slice of bread to create a depression. Place the slices in the prepared air-fryer basket or sheet pan. Pour equal parts of the egg mixture onto the center of each bread slice.

4. *If using an air fryer,* air-fry at 365°F for 6 to 7 minutes for a softer, just-set omelet or 8 to 10 minutes for a fully set omelet. Top with the cheese and air-fry at 375°F for 1 minute to melt the cheese.

If using the oven, bake for 10 to 13 minutes for a softer, just-set omelet or 15 to 18 minutes for a fully set omelet. Top with the cheese and bake for 3 minutes more, or until the cheese has melted.

5. Garnish with green onions, if desired, and enjoy. Best served fresh but can be refrigerated for up to 3 days. To reheat, microwave on high for 30 seconds.

ALLERGENS

NOTE: To make this dish gluten-free, use gluten-free bread.

BLUEBERRY CRISP

OPTION

YIELD: 2 servings   **PREP TIME:** 15 minutes
COOK TIME: 8 to 20 minutes, depending on method

Sometimes when I wake up, I crave something sweet for breakfast. And when that happens, this is my go-to recipe. This blueberry crisp is one of the first breakfast dishes I learned to make, and it cemented my love of cooking. Hopefully you will like it as much as I do! I like to serve it with Greek yogurt to add some protein.

BLUEBERRY FILLING

1 cup frozen blueberries, defrosted

3 tablespoons honey

1 teaspoon ground cinnamon

CRUMBLE TOPPING

⅔ cup rolled oats

1½ tablespoons refined coconut oil, melted

¼ cup honey

1 teaspoon ground cinnamon

½ teaspoon vanilla extract

½ cup vanilla-flavored Greek yogurt, for serving (optional)

1. *If using the toaster oven or oven,* preheat it to 375°F.

2. In a 7½ by 6-inch baking dish, mix together the blueberries, honey, and cinnamon. Using a fork, mash the ingredients until about half of the blueberries are crushed.

3. In a medium-sized mixing bowl, stir the oats, coconut oil, honey, cinnamon, and vanilla until well combined. Top the blueberry mixture with the crumble mixture.

4. Air-fry at 360°F for 8 to 10 minutes or bake in the oven for 15 to 20 minutes, until the crumble topping starts to brown. Remove and allow to cool slightly before eating.

5. If desired, enjoy each serving with ¼ cup of yogurt. Best served fresh but can last in the fridge for up to 4 days. To reheat, microwave on high for 1 minute.

NOTES: If gluten is an issue for you, be sure to purchase oats labeled gluten-free. Some oats can have trace amounts of gluten if processed in a facility that also processes grains with gluten content.

To make this dish dairy-free, serve the crisp on its own or with a dairy-free yogurt.

If you don't have a 7½ by 6-inch or similar-sized baking dish, you can make this recipe in two 4-ounce ramekins or other oven-safe bowls.

ALLERGENS

OPTION

CINNAMON APPLE CHEESECAKE PROTEIN PARFAIT

OPTION

YIELD: 1 serving   **PREP TIME:** 5 minutes, plus overnight to chill (optional)

With its maple, cinnamon, and apple flavors, this is a perfect recipe for fall, but you can have it whenever you like! This parfait can be enjoyed right away or after setting up in the fridge overnight. I make it in the morning since I like it right after it's assembled, but I will admit the filling does become thicker and more cheesecake-like after chilling for several hours. Totally up to you on that!

½ cup granola

1 cup vanilla-flavored Greek yogurt

2 tablespoons sugar-free cheesecake-flavored pudding mix

1 tablespoon maple syrup

½ teaspoon ground cinnamon, plus more for garnish

1 small apple, for garnish

1. Pour the granola into a 12-ounce jar, short glass, or serving bowl.

2. In a medium-sized mixing bowl, stir together the yogurt, pudding mix, maple syrup, and cinnamon. Spoon the mixture on top of the granola, then dust with more cinnamon. (Or, for a slightly fancier presentation, as shown, make layers: granola, "cheesecake," granola, "cheesecake," granola.)

3. Enjoy right away or place in the fridge to chill overnight. Just before serving, chop or slice the apple and place it on top of the cheesecake mixture.

ALLERGENS

NOTE: To make this parfait gluten-free, use granola labeled gluten-free to avoid oats that have been cross-contaminated with gluten-containing products during processing.

BAKED SPICED PEACH

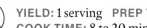 **YIELD:** 1 serving   **PREP TIME:** 10 minutes
COOK TIME: 8 to 20 minutes, depending on method

Peaches are among the most versatile fruits. They are perfect in salads, sandwiches, desserts, and breakfasts. This refreshing peach recipe will fill you with energy and leave you feeling satisfied. I enjoy it with vanilla yogurt to add protein and creaminess, but that is totally optional! To save time, I use my air fryer for this recipe, but if you don't have one, you can bake the peach in the oven or toaster oven.

1 peach

½ cup rolled oats

2 tablespoons maple syrup

1½ teaspoons refined coconut oil, melted

½ teaspoon ground cinnamon, plus more for garnish if desired

¼ cup vanilla-flavored Greek yogurt, for serving (optional)

1. *If using the toaster oven or oven,* preheat it to 375°F.

2. Slice the peach in half, remove the pit, and put the halves in a small baking dish, cut side up.

3. In a small bowl, mix the oats, maple syrup, coconut oil, and cinnamon until well combined.

4. Mound the oat mixture on top of the peach halves, dividing it equally between them and pressing it into the cavities.

5. Air-fry at 365°F for 8 to 10 minutes or bake in the oven for 15 to 20 minutes, until the oats turn golden brown. If desired, top with yogurt and an extra sprinkle of cinnamon.

ALLERGENS

OPTION

NOTES: If gluten is an issue for you, be sure to purchase oats labeled gluten-free. To make this dish vegan or dairy-free, use a vegan yogurt or omit the yogurt altogether.

PROTEIN BROWNIE BALLS

   YIELD: 3 to 4 servings (2 or 3 balls per serving)   **PREP TIME:** 15 minutes

Make these brownie balls one night before bed and you'll have breakfast for three days—or a great snack to take along on a road trip! I usually eat two or three on a busy weekday morning when I am in a rush or when I lack the energy to make a "real" breakfast. They are easy to transport and full of protein, fiber, and fat to keep you full for hours.

1 cup finely ground blanched almond flour

¼ cup cocoa powder

1 scoop chocolate-flavored protein powder

Pinch of salt

½ cup chunky natural peanut butter

½ cup maple syrup

Dark chocolate chips, to taste

1. Dump all of the ingredients into a large bowl and mix until well combined.

2. Roll the mixture into nine 1-inch balls and enjoy! They will last in the fridge for up to a week.

NOTE: To make these brownie balls vegan, use a vegan protein powder. (Some protein powders are made from whey or egg.) To make them dairy-free, use a dairy-free protein powder and dairy-free chocolate chips.

ALLERGENS

OPTION

PEACH CUSTARD OATS

OPTION

YIELD: 1 serving **PREP TIME:** 15 minutes, plus overnight to chill if desired

Much like the Cinnamon Apple Cheesecake Protein Parfait on page 50, this dish is equally great right after it's made or after being chilled in the fridge overnight. To me, it brings to mind a calm, sunny late summer morning. It is filling and refreshing and has the perfect balance of complex carbs, protein, and other nutrients to keep you nourished throughout the morning!

½ cup rolled oats

1 teaspoon sugar-free vanilla-flavored pudding mix

¼ teaspoon ground cinnamon

⅔ cup milk of choice

¼ cup vanilla-flavored Greek yogurt

2 teaspoons honey, plus more for garnish

1 peach

3 tablespoons chopped roasted pecans, for garnish

1. In a 12-ounce serving bowl, mix the oats, pudding mix, cinnamon, milk, yogurt, and honey until well combined.

2. Slice half of the peach and set aside for garnish. Dice the other half of the peach and stir it into the oat mixture.

3. To serve, drizzle with honey, then top with the pecans and garnish with the peach slices. Eat right away or, if you prefer, refrigerate overnight to create a thicker, creamier texture.

ALLERGENS

NOTE: If gluten is an issue for you, be sure to purchase oats labeled gluten-free.

ANY BERRY FRENCH TOAST MUFFINS

OPTION

YIELD: 4 muffins   **PREP TIME:** 10 minutes   **COOK TIME:** 20 minutes

This is a fun little breakfast treat that my mom used to make for me when I was little. Instead of standing at a stovetop for half an hour flipping French toast, you just fill the muffin cups and bake them. You can use any type of fruit you want, but I prefer frozen berries, especially blueberries. If you do not like or have berries, diced apple would be the second-best choice for this recipe.

6 slices whole wheat bread

2 large eggs

⅔ cup milk of choice

½ teaspoon ground cinnamon

½ teaspoon vanilla extract

½ to ⅔ cup frozen berries of choice

1. Preheat the toaster oven or oven to 350°F. Line four wells of a standard-sized muffin pan with paper liners.

2. Tear the bread into 1-inch pieces and put in a medium-sized bowl; set aside.

3. In a separate medium-sized bowl, mix the eggs, milk, cinnamon, and vanilla until well combined. Pour the egg mixture into the bowl with the bread pieces and lightly fold the bread and egg mixture together. Spoon the French toast mixture evenly into the prepared wells of the muffin pan, filling each about three-quarters full.

4. Top with the frozen berries. If using frozen strawberries, dice them before topping.

5. Bake for 15 to 20 minutes, until the muffins are starting to brown around the edges. Remove from the pan and let cool slightly before eating. Best served fresh, but leftovers can be refrigerated for up to 5 days. To reheat, microwave on medium-high for 30 seconds.

NOTE: To make these muffins gluten-free, use gluten-free bread. To make them dairy-free, use a plant-based milk.

CAKE FOR BREAKFAST

OPTION

YIELD: 1 serving   **PREP TIME:** 10 minutes   **COOK TIME:** 20 minutes

I love this rich and filling cake when I have a major sweet tooth in the morning. I always dreamed of having dessert for breakfast, and here it is! It is a little comfort meal for your inner child. This recipe is super versatile; I like chocolate and peanut butter, but you can change up the flavors. If you own a blender and prefer to use rolled oats, use the blender variation below the recipe—a quick whizz until mostly smooth, and the batter is ready.

½ ripe banana

1 large egg, beaten

¼ cup milk of choice

1½ tablespoons honey

½ teaspoon vanilla extract

½ cup oat flour

½ teaspoon baking powder

¼ teaspoon ground cinnamon

½ cup dark chocolate chunks

FOR THE TOP

½ cup milk of choice, warmed (optional)

1 tablespoon natural peanut butter

1. Preheat the toaster oven or oven to 350°F. Grease an 8-ounce ramekin or other oven-safe bowl with cooking oil spray.

2. In a small bowl, mash the banana with a fork until smooth. Add the egg, milk, honey, and vanilla and stir until well combined.

3. In a medium-sized bowl, whisk together the oat flour, baking powder, and cinnamon. Pour the wet ingredients into the dry ingredients and stir until well combined.

4. Pour the batter into the prepared ramekin or bowl, then gently fold in the chocolate chunks.

5. Bake for 15 to 20 minutes, until a toothpick comes out with moist crumbs when inserted in the center of the cake.

6. For a tres leches–style cake, use a toothpick to poke five or six holes in the cake, then pour the warm milk over the cake.

7. Dollop the peanut butter on top of the cake and let it melt. Once melted, spread it evenly across the top with a spoon and enjoy!

Rolled oats blender variation: Put the first eight ingredients, replacing the oat flour with rolled oats, in a blender and blend until mostly smooth. Complete the recipe as written, picking up at Step 4.

NOTE: To make this cake gluten-free, use gluten-free oat flour (or rolled oats) to avoid oat flour (or oats) that during processing has been cross-contaminated with other products containing gluten. To make it dairy-free, use a plant-based milk and vegan chocolate.

ALLERGENS

OPTION

PUMPKIN SPICE FRENCH TOAST BITES

OPTION

YIELD: 1 serving   **PREP TIME:** 5 minutes
COOK TIME: 5 to 25 minutes, depending on method

I don't know about you, but I enjoy pumpkin spice all year round. If you are like me, then you will love this easy, fail-proof recipe. It will put you in the fall mood every time, no matter what season it is! I prefer to air-fry the bites, but a toaster oven or a hot pan works well too.

3 slices whole wheat bread (preferably Texas toast style)

1 large egg, beaten

½ cup milk of choice

½ teaspoon vanilla extract

½ teaspoon pumpkin pie spice

Maple syrup, for serving

1. *If using the toaster oven or oven,* preheat it to 350°F. Line a small sheet pan with parchment paper.

If using an air fryer, line the air-fryer basket with parchment paper.

2. Cut each slice of bread into thirds, to make a total of nine strips.

3. In a medium-sized bowl, mix the egg, milk, vanilla, and pumpkin pie spice until well combined. Dip the bread strips into the egg mixture.

4. *If using an air fryer,* place the coated strips in the prepared air-fryer basket and air-fry at 365°F for 5 to 8 minutes, until golden brown.

If using the oven, place the strips on the prepared sheet pan and bake for 10 to 15 minutes, then flip and bake for 10 minutes more, or until golden brown.

If using a hot plate or the stovetop, fry the strips in a medium-sized greased frying pan over medium-high heat for 5 minutes, or until golden brown. Flip and fry for 5 minutes more, or until golden brown on both sides.

5. Enjoy the bites with maple syrup.

ALLERGENS

OPTION

NOTE: To make these bites gluten-free, use gluten-free bread. To make them dairy-free, use a plant-based milk.

PB & BANANA QUESADILLA

OPTION

YIELD: 1 serving   **PREP TIME:** 5 minutes
COOK TIME: 8 to 18 minutes, depending on method

This is one of the first breakfasts I made when I was living in a college dorm. The reason I love this recipe so much and put it in this book is because it is so easy to make, anyone anywhere can cook it, and it keeps you full for hours thanks to the high-fiber wheat and heart-healthy fats. It is perfect when on the run or for a late-night snack.

2 tablespoons natural peanut butter

2 (10-inch) whole wheat flour tortillas

1 banana

1 tablespoon honey

2 teaspoons unsweetened shredded coconut, plus more or garnish if desired

½ teaspoon ground cinnamon

1. *If using the toaster oven or oven,* preheat it to 375°F and line a small sheet pan with parchment paper.

   If using an air fryer, line the air-fryer basket with parchment paper.

2. Smear the peanut butter on one side of each tortilla.

3. Cut the banana into ¼-inch slices, then place the slices on top of the peanut butter on one tortilla. Drizzle with the honey, then sprinkle with the shredded coconut and cinnamon. Place the second tortilla on top, peanut butter side down.

4. Place the quesadilla in the prepared basket or sheet pan. Lightly coat the quesadilla with cooking oil spray.

5. *If using an air fryer,* air-fry at 360°F for 8 minutes, or until golden brown.

   If using the oven, bake the quesadilla for 10 to 13 minutes, or until it turns lightly golden brown, then flip and bake for 5 minutes more, or until golden brown on both sides.

6. Cut into four slices, sprinkle with shredded coconut, if desired, and enjoy!

ALLERGENS

NOTE: To make this quesadilla gluten-free, use gluten-free tortillas.

NO-BAKE EVERYTHING BREAKFAST BARS

  YIELD: 8 bars (2 per serving)   **PREP TIME:** 10 minutes, plus overnight to set up

OPTION   OPTION

I created this no-bake recipe one day when I was craving granola bars but didn't want to go shopping for them. So I gathered a bunch of ingredients from my pantry that I thought would be great in a granola bar—basically everything but the kitchen sink—and combined them. Fortunately, this made one of the best granola bars I have ever had!

2 cups rolled oats

1 cup natural peanut butter

⅔ cup maple syrup

¼ cup sliced almonds

¼ cup dark chocolate chips

¼ cup unsweetened shredded coconut, plus more for the top

¼ cup mini-twist pretzels

¼ cup sweetened dried cranberries

Pinch of salt

1. Line the bottom and sides of a 9-inch square baking dish with parchment paper.

2. In a medium-sized bowl, mix all of the ingredients until well combined.

3. Transfer the mixture to the prepared pan. Using your hands, press the mixture into an even layer across the bottom of the pan, spreading it to the corners. Sprinkle with shredded coconut, then cut into eight bars.

4. Refrigerate overnight to solidify the mixture, then enjoy the next morning! The bars can last in the fridge for up to 1 week.

ALLERGENS

NOTE: To make these bars vegan, use vegan chocolate chips. If gluten is an issue for you, be sure to purchase oats labeled gluten-free. Some oats can have trace amounts of gluten if processed in a facility that also processes grains with gluten content.

CREAM CHEESE & JAM FRENCH TOAST ROLL-UPS

OPTION

YIELD: 1 serving   **PREP TIME:** 10 minutes
COOK TIME: 3 to 10 minutes, depending on method

When I started to get creative in the kitchen, this was one of the first recipes I developed. These super simple roll-ups will satisfy any sweet tooth, no matter how strong. I like to eat them as-is, but they are also enjoyable when drizzled with honey or maple syrup. I make them in an air fryer, but if you don't have one, you can cook them in a frying pan.

3 slices whole wheat bread

1½ tablespoons ⅓-less-fat cream cheese (aka Neufchâtel), softened

1½ tablespoons strawberry jam

1 large egg, beaten

½ cup milk of choice

½ teaspoon vanilla extract

½ teaspoon ground cinnamon

Powdered sugar, for garnish (optional)

Maple syrup or honey, for serving (optional)

1. Cut the crust off the bread and flatten the slices with a rolling pin.

2. Spread one-third of the cream cheese, then one-third of the jam, on one side of each slice of bread. Roll up the bread slices.

3. In a medium-sized bowl, mix together the egg, milk, vanilla, and cinnamon until well combined. Coat the bread roll-ups in the egg mixture.

4. Place the roll-ups seam side down in the air-fryer basket or in a medium-sized greased frying pan. Air-fry at 350°F for 8 minutes or pan-fry over medium-high heat for 3 to 5 minutes, until the roll-ups are golden brown on all sides.

5. Enjoy as-is or dust with powdered sugar. Serve with maple syrup or honey on the side, if desired.

ALLERGENS

NOTE: To make these roll-ups gluten-free, use gluten-free bread.

MICROWAVE CRANBERRY PECAN BREAKFAST COOKIE

YIELD: 1 serving   **PREP TIME:** 10 minutes   **COOK TIME:** 1 minute

Ever crave a breakfast cookie but don't have time on a busy morning to make a full batch and wait for them to bake? Well, this recipe is for those mornings. Just mix the ingredients in a microwave-safe bowl, microwave for a minute, and you have your own individual breakfast cookie—fast and easy! If you're looking for an indulgent breakfast, be sure to include the white chocolate chips; they add a touch of extra sweetness and a wonderful creaminess.

1 tablespoon unsweetened applesauce

2 teaspoons vegetable oil

1 teaspoon maple syrup

1 teaspoon brown sugar

½ teaspoon vanilla extract

¼ cup quick oats

1 tablespoon all-purpose flour

¼ teaspoon baking powder

Pinch of ground cinnamon

Pinch of salt

1 tablespoon sweetened dried cranberries

1 tablespoon chopped raw pecans

1 tablespoon white chocolate chips (optional)

1. In a small microwave-safe bowl that's about 5 inches in diameter and 2 inches deep, mix together the applesauce, vegetable oil, maple syrup, brown sugar, and vanilla until well combined.

2. Stir in the oats, flour, baking powder, cinnamon, and salt until well combined.

3. Fold in the cranberries, pecans, and white chocolate chips, if using.

4. Microwave on high for 1 minute, or until the center is cooked. Enjoy with a spoon, directly out of the bowl.

ALLERGENS

NOTE: To make this cookie vegan and dairy-free, use vegan white chocolate chips or omit them altogether.

S'MORES PROTEIN COOKIE

OPTION OPTION OPTION

YIELD: 1 serving **PREP TIME:** 10 minutes
COOK TIME: 8 to 13 minutes, depending on method

I just love s'mores. How could you go wrong with the perfect combination of chocolate, marshmallow, and graham crackers? You don't have to confine the trio to the classic bonfire treat (although, in my opinion, it's one of the best parts of summer); here I've used the s'more as the basis for a breakfast cookie. This cookie works just as well for dessert as it does for breakfast. Why limit yourself?

½ medium ripe banana

⅔ cup rolled oats

1 scoop vanilla-flavored protein powder

1½ tablespoons olive oil

1 tablespoon milk of choice

½ teaspoon vanilla extract

¼ teaspoon baking powder

Pinch of salt

2 tablespoons dark chocolate chips

2 tablespoons mini marshmallows

1 tablespoon coarsely crushed graham crackers

1. *If using a toaster oven or oven,* preheat it to 375°F and line a small sheet pan with parchment paper.

If using an air fryer, line the air-fryer basket with parchment paper.

2. In a medium-sized mixing bowl, mash the banana with a fork until it has the texture of a puree. Add the oats, protein powder, olive oil, milk, vanilla, baking powder, and salt and mix until well combined. Fold in the chocolate chips, marshmallows, and graham crackers until evenly distributed.

3. Scrape the dough onto the center of the prepared basket or sheet pan and, using a spoon, shape it into a 4-inch round cookie. Air-fry at 350°F for 8 to 10 minutes or bake in the oven for 10 to 13 minutes, until slightly golden brown. Let cool slightly before enjoying.

NOTE: To make this cookie vegetarian, use vegan marshmallows. To make it vegan, use plant-based protein powder and milk, vegan marshmallows, and vegan chocolate chips; to make it dairy-free, use a plant-based milk, nondairy protein powder, and vegan chocolate chips. To make it egg-free, use a protein powder that is not made from egg whites. To make it gluten-free, use gluten-free graham crackers and be sure to purchase oats labeled gluten-free. Some oats can have trace amounts of gluten if processed in a facility that also processes grains with gluten content.

ALLERGENS

OPTION OPTION

SIMPLE BREAKFASTS SWEET

chapter 2:

EFFORTLESS LUNCHES

Lunchtime is my favorite part of the day! This chapter is full of tasty lunches that will keep you satiated and nourished for hours. These lunches saw me through my busy and broke days as a dietetic intern and full-time graduate student. All these recipes are designed to help you prepare midday meals quickly and with little effort. Some, like the slow cooker recipes, can be made ahead and packed in a to-go container in the morning. Feel free to adjust the seasonings and even the ingredients to your liking!

THE ROCKSTAR

YIELD: 2 servings   **PREP TIME:** 10 minutes (not including time to cook chicken)
COOK TIME: 15 minutes to 4 hours, depending on method

This soup earned its name due to its spice level, big flavor, and the shape of the pasta that is used. Inspired by classic chicken noodle soup, its key ingredients are celery, onions, and, of course, chicken, but with a spicy and creamy twist. This soup can be made either in a saucepan or in a slow cooker.

4 cups chicken broth

½ cup chopped red bell peppers

½ cup chopped celery

½ cup chopped yellow onions

1 teaspoon minced garlic

1 teaspoon crushed red pepper

¾ cup shredded cooked chicken breast (see Notes)

⅔ cup half-and-half or unsweetened canned coconut cream

½ cup pastina (aka star pasta) (see Notes)

1 tablespoon dried parsley

1 tablespoon chili oil

1. *To cook the soup on a hot plate or the stovetop,* put the broth, bell peppers, celery, onions, garlic, and crushed red pepper in a medium-sized saucepan and bring to a low boil over medium-high heat, about 10 minutes.

2. Add the chicken, half-and-half, pastina, parsley, and chili oil to the pan. Turn the heat to medium-low and let the soup simmer for 5 minutes, or until the vegetables have softened, the pasta is tender, and the chicken is heated through.

3. *To cook the soup in a slow cooker,* put the broth, bell peppers, celery, onions, garlic, and crushed red pepper in the slow cooker. Cook for 1 hour on high or for 2 hours on low.

4. Add the chicken, half-and-half, pastina, parsley, and chili oil to the slow cooker. Cook for another hour on high or 2 hours on low, or until the vegetables have softened, the pasta is tender, and the chicken is heated through.

5. Ladle into bowls and enjoy! Best served fresh but can last in the fridge for up to 4 days. To reheat, microwave on high for 1 minute.

ALLERGENS

OPTION

NOTE: To make this soup dairy-free, use coconut cream rather than half-and-half.

NOTES: If you do not have leftover cooked chicken breast on hand, you can cook a boneless, skinless chicken breast (about 6 ounces) for use in this soup. If using the stovetop, put the chicken and broth in a medium-sized saucepan. Bring to a boil, then cover, lower the heat to maintain a rapid simmer, and cook until done, about 10 minutes. (To verify doneness, check with a meat thermometer; it should read 165°F.) Shred the chicken and set it aside for Step 2. Complete the recipe as written, using the cooking broth for Step 1.

If using a slow cooker, put the chicken and broth in the slow cooker. Cook for 1 hour on high or 2 hours on low, then add the rest of the ingredients listed in Step 3. After cooking for another 1 hour on high or 2 hours on low, remove the chicken and shred it, then complete Step 4.

Pastina is a tiny star-shaped pasta. If you have trouble finding it, you can substitute orzo. Either type is available gluten-free.

To make this soup dairy-free, use coconut cream instead of half-and-half.

FAUX PHO

OPTION

YIELD: 1 serving   **PREP TIME:** 10 minutes   **COOK TIME:** 6 minutes

This was a frequent meal prep for me when I was working in a hospital. I would pack all the ingredients into a microwave-safe container, add the water when it was time to eat, and microwave it. Then, BOOM—I had a balanced and nutritious meal! This recipe is great even if you are looking for a nutritious lunch at home. You can think of it as a better-for-you homemade version of a packaged dry soup mix. Traditional pho takes much longer to make than this "faux" version and includes a much longer list of ingredients; if you'd like to make this recipe a bit closer to an authentic pho without much effort, add one star anise or one whole clove in Step 1 and a splash of fish sauce in Step 2, removing the whole spice before serving.

2 ounces vermicelli rice noodles

½ cup frozen precooked small shrimp

¼ cup shaved carrots

¼ cup sliced mushrooms of choice

¼ cup sliced sugar snap peas

1 chicken bouillon cube (see Notes)

1 tablespoon olive oil

1 tablespoon soy sauce

½ teaspoon ginger powder

¼ teaspoon garlic powder

2 cups water

FOR SERVING

1 hard-boiled egg, sliced in half

1 lime wedge (optional)

Sriracha sauce (optional)

ALLERGENS

OPTION

1. Put the rice noodles, shrimp, carrots, mushrooms, and sugar snap peas in a medium-sized microwave-safe bowl.

2. Add the bouillon cube, olive oil, soy sauce, ginger powder, and garlic powder, then pour in the water and stir to combine.

3. Place a microwave-safe plate on top of the bowl and microwave on medium-high for 6 minutes, or until the noodles are soft and the vegetables are tender. Serve topped with the egg halves and, if desired, a squeeze of lime juice and/or a squirt of Sriracha.

NOTES: I use a chicken bouillon cube to make this soup extra transportable and convenient to prepare no matter where you are. If you don't have a bouillon cube on hand, you can omit it and replace the water with chicken broth.

To make this soup gluten-free, make sure to buy gluten-free rice noodles and use gluten-free soy sauce or tamari. To make it egg-free, leave out the hard-boiled egg.

SPICY DUMPLING NOODLE SOUP

OPTION OPTION

YIELD: 1 serving   **PREP TIME:** 5 minutes   **COOK TIME:** 6 minutes

Just like the Faux Pho on page 78, this quick and easy Asian-inspired meal was one of my favorites when I was completing my dietetic internship, and I still make it regularly today. It is perfectly balanced, nutritious, and soul- and mouth-warming. I like to use veggie or chicken dumplings, but feel free to use pork ones if you prefer. Note that this soup is spicy; if you'd like a milder soup, simply adjust to your preferred spice level.

2 ounces glass noodles or vermicelli rice noodles

4 or 5 premade frozen dumplings (aka potstickers or gyoza)

½ cup chopped bok choy

½ cup frozen broccoli florets

2 cups vegetable broth

½ teaspoon dried minced onions

½ teaspoon crushed red pepper

¼ teaspoon ginger powder

1 tablespoon toasted sesame oil

1 teaspoon chili oil

1. Put the rice noodles, dumplings, bok choy, and broccoli in a medium-sized microwave-safe bowl.

2. Add the broth, dried minced onions, crushed red pepper, ginger powder, sesame oil, and chili oil and stir to combine.

3. Place a microwave-safe plate on top of the bowl and microwave on medium-high for 6 minutes, or until the noodles are soft, the dumplings are thoroughly cooked, and the broccoli is tender. Enjoy!

NOTE: To make this soup vegetarian or vegan, use vegan dumplings.

EVERYTHING BUT THE KITCHEN SINK SOUP

 YIELD: 3 servings   **PREP TIME:** 10 minutes (not including time to cook chicken)
COOK TIME: 18 minutes

When I'm at a loss for what to do with the odd bits I have in my fridge and pantry, this soup is my go-to meal. The first time I made it, I immediately fell in love because it is super flavorful and kept me feeling full and nourished. These are the ingredients I tend to use, but feel free to adjust them to what's available in your kitchen. Just keep with the main concept: some broth, meat, beans, vegetables, and seasonings.

3 cups chicken broth

2 tablespoons olive oil

½ cup chopped smoked sausage (see Note)

½ cup shredded cooked chicken breast

½ cup chopped carrots

½ cup chopped red bell peppers

½ cup chopped yellow onions

½ cup canned cannellini beans, rinsed and drained

1 teaspoon dried parsley

½ teaspoon garlic powder

1. Pour the broth and olive oil into a medium-sized saucepan, then add the sausage and chicken. Bring to a low boil over medium-high heat, then reduce the heat to a simmer and cook for another 5 minutes.

2. Add the carrots, bell peppers, onions, beans, dried parsley, and garlic powder and simmer for another 10 minutes, or until the vegetables are tender.

3. Ladle into bowls and enjoy! Best served fresh but can last in the fridge for up to 4 days. To reheat, microwave on high for 1 minute.

NOTE: You can use any smoked sausage you prefer. I used Hillshire Farms Beef Smoked Sausage.

SPICY EGG DROP SOUP

 YIELD: 1 serving   **PREP TIME:** 5 minutes   **COOK TIME:** 10 minutes

Egg drop soup initially appeared on the must-test list for this book because it is cheap and easy to make. At first I thought I wouldn't like it, but as it turns out, this is a terrific recipe! My version is inspired by traditional egg drop soup, but I added some spice to it, along with some cheese to give it extra protein, calcium, and flavor. It may sound like an odd combination, but it came out great!

2 cups chicken broth

½ teaspoon cornstarch

1 teaspoon water

2 tablespoons sliced green onions

1 tablespoon chili oil

⅛ teaspoon garlic powder

⅛ teaspoon ginger powder

1 large egg

¼ cup shredded cheddar cheese (optional)

1. Bring the broth to a boil in a medium-sized saucepan over high heat.

2. While the broth is heating, make a cornstarch slurry by stirring the cornstarch and water together until the cornstarch has dissolved.

3. Once the broth is at a boil, slowly stir in the cornstarch slurry, then add the green onions, chili oil, garlic powder, and ginger powder. Whisk the egg, then slowly drizzle it into the boiling broth while stirring.

4. Once the egg is cooked, add the cheese, if using, and let it melt. Ladle the soup into a bowl and enjoy.

ALLERGENS

OPTION

NOTE: To make this soup dairy-free, omit the cheese.

MY FAVORITE GOURMET SALAD

 YIELD: 1 serving   **PREP TIME:** 15 minutes   **COOK TIME:** 12 to 25 minutes, depending on method

When I was a freshman in college, I worked at a little family-owned deli that made the absolute best salads and sandwiches. My best friend worked there too, and one day she whipped up this gourmet medley for me, which immediately became my all-time favorite salad. It has the perfect balance of sweet, salty, and tangy flavors. I hope you enjoy it as much as I do!

CHICKEN

1 small boneless, skinless chicken breast (about 4 ounces)

1 tablespoon olive oil

½ teaspoon garlic powder

½ teaspoon paprika

½ teaspoon rubbed dried sage

Pinch of salt

Pinch of ground black pepper

RASPBERRY VINAIGRETTE

3 tablespoons extra-virgin olive oil

1 tablespoon raspberry jam

1 tablespoon red wine vinegar

1 tablespoon lemon juice

Pinch of salt

Pinch of ground black pepper

SALAD

3 cups spring mix

¼ cup sweetened dried cranberries

¼ cup salted roasted pistachios (without shells)

¼ cup crumbled blue cheese

1. *If using the toaster oven or oven,* preheat it to 375°F and line a small sheet pan with aluminum foil. *If using an air fryer,* line the air-fryer basket with foil.

2. Coat the chicken breast with the olive oil, sprinkle it with the garlic powder, paprika, sage, salt, and pepper, then rub in the seasonings.

3. Set the chicken in the prepared air-fryer basket or sheet pan. Air-fry at 375°F for 12 to 15 minutes or bake in the oven for 20 to 25 minutes, until fully cooked. To test doneness, insert a meat thermometer in the thickest part of the breast; when done, the internal temperature will have reached 165°F. The chicken should be tender and juicy.

4. Let the chicken rest for 2 minutes, then cut it into strips.

5. In a small bowl, whisk together the ingredients for the vinaigrette until well combined.

6. Put the spring mix, cranberries, pistachios, and blue cheese in a serving bowl. Drizzle the vinaigrette over the salad and top with the chicken. Toss and enjoy!

ALLERGENS

SUNSHINE IN A BOWL

  YIELD: 1 serving   **PREP TIME:** 10 minutes

What do you think of when you think of sunshine? I usually think of spring and summer, which is often the best time of year when it comes to salads. Many fruits and vegetables are at their peak of flavor, especially strawberries and tender young spinach. No matter what season it is, this salad will transport you to those beautiful sunshiny days.

3 cups fresh spinach

½ small avocado, diced

¼ cup sliced strawberries

¼ cup fresh clementine slices or drained canned mandarin oranges

¼ cup crumbled fresh (soft) goat cheese

¼ cup raw walnuts

¼ cup hulled hemp seeds

DRESSING

2 tablespoons extra-virgin olive oil

1 tablespoon red wine vinegar

1 tablespoon orange juice

1½ teaspoons honey

1 tablespoon chopped fresh parsley

Pinch of salt

Pinch of ground black pepper

1. In a serving bowl, gently toss the spinach, avocado, strawberries, clementine slices, goat cheese, walnuts, and hemp seeds until evenly distributed.

2. In a small bowl, whisk together the ingredients for the dressing until well combined.

3. Drizzle the dressing over the salad and enjoy!

ALLERGENS

TOASTED CHICKPEA SALAD

YIELD: 1 serving **PREP TIME:** 10 minutes (not including time to cook chicken) **COOK TIME:** 15 minutes

Looking for a fun recipe? You're welcome! Not only is this salad full of fiber, protein, and vitamins, but it is also very filling—a real hunger crusher. It is warm not only temperature-wise but also flavor-wise. I like the toasted chickpeas extra spicy, but feel free to dial down the quantity of hot sauce to your liking.

SPICY TOASTED CHICKPEAS

½ cup canned chickpeas, rinsed and drained

1 tablespoon medium-hot hot sauce, such as Frank's RedHot Original

1 tablespoon olive oil

1 teaspoon garlic powder

½ cup shredded cooked chicken breast

¼ cup diced red onions

¼ cup chopped celery

¼ cup chopped yellow or red bell peppers

2 cups chopped lettuce

2 tablespoons lemon juice

1 tablespoon extra-virgin olive oil

Salt and pepper

1. Preheat the toaster oven or oven to 375°F.

2. Pat the chickpeas dry with a paper towel, then put them in a medium-sized bowl. Add the hot sauce, olive oil, and garlic powder and toss until the chickpeas are well coated. Pour onto a small sheet pan; set the bowl aside.

3. Bake the chickpeas for 10 to 15 minutes, or until toasted and slightly golden. Transfer the toasted chickpeas back to the bowl.

4. To the bowl with the chickpeas, add the chicken, onions, celery, and bell peppers. Mix until evenly distributed.

5. Put the lettuce in a serving bowl, then drizzle with the lemon juice and olive oil. Season to taste with salt and pepper and toss until the lettuce is evenly coated.

6. Pour the chickpea and chicken mixture over the dressed lettuce and enjoy!

NOTE: To make this salad vegetarian or vegan, omit the chicken.

WARM CHICKEN & KALE SALAD

YIELD: 1 serving   PREP TIME: 10 minutes   COOK TIME: 12 to 25 minutes, depending on method

Chicken goes with just about everything, but it is especially great in a salad. Something about chicken smothered in a flavorful dressing makes my mouth water. This protein-rich and fiber-packed salad will keep you full and focused until dinnertime!

1 small boneless, skinless chicken breast (about 4 ounces)

½ teaspoon paprika

½ teaspoon garlic powder

½ teaspoon onion powder

Pinch of salt

Pinch of ground black pepper

¼ cup water

¼ cup couscous

1 cup torn kale leaves

¼ cup diced tomatoes

¼ cup diced red onions

¼ cup crumbled feta cheese

DRESSING

2 tablespoons extra-virgin olive oil

3 tablespoons red wine vinegar

1 teaspoon Italian seasoning

1 teaspoon dried minced onions

1 teaspoon minced garlic

½ teaspoon crushed red pepper

Pinch of salt

Pinch of ground black pepper

ALLERGENS

1. *If using the toaster oven or oven,* preheat it to 375°F and line a small sheet pan with aluminum foil. *If using an air fryer,* line the air-fryer basket with foil.

2. Sprinkle the chicken breast with the paprika, garlic powder, onion powder, salt, and pepper, then rub the seasonings into the meat.

3. Place the chicken in the prepared air-fryer basket or sheet pan and air-fry at 375°F for 12 to 15 minutes or bake in the oven for 20 to 25 minutes, until fully cooked. To test doneness, insert a meat thermometer in the thickest part of the breast; when done, the internal temperature will have reached 165°F. The chicken should be tender and juicy. While the chicken is cooking, prepare the rest of the ingredients, starting with the couscous.

4. Pour the water into a medium-sized microwave-safe bowl. Cover the bowl with a microwave-safe plate and microwave on high for 3 minutes, or until the water is boiling. Once at a boil, stir in the couscous and cover again. Let sit for about 5 minutes, until the couscous has absorbed all the water and softened, then fluff the couscous with a fork.

5. Put the kale in a serving bowl and massage for 1 minute to soften the leaves. Add the tomatoes, onions, feta, and couscous and toss gently to combine.

6. When the chicken is done, remove it from the air fryer or oven and let it rest for 2 minutes, then cut it into strips. Lay the chicken strips on top of the salad.

7. In a small bowl, whisk together the ingredients for the dressing until well combined.

8. Drizzle the dressing on the salad, toss, and enjoy!

HEARTY VEGETARIAN BOWL

  YIELD: 1 serving   **PREP TIME:** 10 minutes

You are in a rush to get to work, or you're strapped for time but still need to make lunch. Does this scenario sound familiar? Well, this recipe is perfect for those times, because all you need to do is throw some ingredients into a bowl. If you prep the vegetables in advance, you'll have this hearty bowl done in a couple of minutes, making it the perfect last-minute meal!

¼ cup canned chickpeas, rinsed and drained

¼ cup canned cannellini beans, rinsed and drained

¼ cup crumbled feta cheese

¼ cup drained canned corn

½ cup quartered grape tomatoes

½ medium avocado, diced

1 tablespoon coarsely chopped fresh cilantro

1½ tablespoons extra-virgin olive oil

2 tablespoons lemon juice

1 tablespoon dried dill weed

½ teaspoon garlic powder

Pinch of salt

Pinch of ground black pepper

1. Put the chickpeas, beans, feta, corn, tomatoes, avocado, and cilantro in a serving bowl.

2. Drizzle the olive oil and lemon juice over the ingredients, then sprinkle on the dill, garlic powder, salt, and pepper.

3. Toss gently until the seasonings are evenly distributed and enjoy.

ALLERGENS

MOM'S COUSCOUS SALAD

 YIELD: 2 servings   **PREP TIME:** 10 minutes   **COOK TIME:** 3 minutes

When I was growing up, my mom made the best salads, and my all-time favorite of hers is this couscous salad. She dresses the couscous with olive oil and orange juice and then adds feta cheese, toasted pine nuts, and fresh vegetables and herbs from her garden. This is a little taste from my home to yours!

⅔ cup water

⅔ cup couscous

2 tablespoons extra-virgin olive oil

2 tablespoons orange juice

1 tablespoon chopped fresh cilantro or parsley

1 tablespoon sliced green onions

Pinch of salt

Pinch of ground black pepper

¼ cup crumbled feta cheese

¼ cup pine nuts (raw or toasted)

¼ cup chopped zucchini

¼ cup diced tomatoes

¼ cup diced yellow bell peppers

3 tablespoons finely diced red onions

1. Pour the water into a medium-sized microwave-safe bowl, then cover the bowl with a microwave-safe plate and microwave on high for 3 minutes, or until the water is boiling. Stir in the couscous and cover again. Let sit for about 5 minutes, until the couscous has absorbed the water and softened. When done, fluff the couscous with a fork.

2. Add the olive oil, orange juice, cilantro, green onions, salt, and black pepper to the bowl with the couscous. Mix well to evenly distribute the dressing.

3. Add the feta, pine nuts, zucchini, tomatoes, bell peppers, and onions and toss until the salad is well mixed. Enjoy immediately or store in the fridge for up to 5 days.

ALLERGENS

CLASSY POTATO SALAD

 YIELD: 1 serving   **PREP TIME:** 10 minutes   **COOK TIME:** 8 to 15 minutes, depending on method

Sometimes mayonnaise doesn't sit right with me. If you are like me, then you will enjoy this mayo-less potato salad that is tossed with smoky bacon—providing protein and great flavor—and is lighter than the more common mayo-based version. I often call this potato salad lunch, enjoying a large bowl of it. Of course, you can also serve it as a side; try it with my BBQ Pulled Chicken Sandwiches on page 192. I call this potato salad "classy" because I think it looks like a version that would be served in a fine-dining restaurant.

1½ cups halved baby red potatoes

4 cups water

Pinch of salt

3 slices turkey bacon

¼ cup diced red onions

DRESSING

3 tablespoons extra-virgin olive oil

2 tablespoons red wine vinegar

1½ teaspoons Dijon mustard

1½ teaspoons dried dill weed

½ teaspoon garlic powder

Crushed red pepper, to taste

Salt and pepper, to taste

1. *If using the toaster oven or oven,* preheat it to 375°F and line a small sheet pan with aluminum foil. *If using an air fryer,* line the air-fryer basked with foil.

2. Put the potatoes in a medium-sized saucepan and cover with the water. Bring the water to a boil, add the salt, and cook at a rapid simmer until the potatoes are fork-tender, about 8 minutes. When the potatoes are done, drain well. Meanwhile, cook the bacon.

3. Place the bacon in the prepared air-fryer basket or sheet pan and air-fry at 350°F for 8 minutes or bake in the oven for 10 to 15 minutes, until slightly crispy. Cut the bacon into bite-sized pieces.

4. In a serving bowl, whisk together the ingredients for the dressing until well combined.

5. Add the potatoes, onions, and bacon to the bowl, mix until evenly distributed, and enjoy!

THE MEDITERRANEAN PASTA SALAD BABY

OPTION

YIELD: 2 servings   **PREP TIME:** 10 minutes   **COOK TIME:** 10 minutes

Two of my favorite types of salad are Mediterranean salads (think Greek salad) and pasta salads, especially ones that showcase savory meats, like ham. They are just so vibrant, flavorful, and packed with nutrients. So, why not combine the two to make an offspring?

Salt

¾ cup bowtie pasta

¼ cup crumbled feta cheese

¼ cup chopped deli ham

¼ cup halved black olives

¼ cup quartered grape tomatoes

¼ cup chopped cucumbers

¼ cup chopped yellow bell peppers

¼ cup Italian dressing of choice

Ground black pepper

1. Fill a medium-sized saucepan halfway with water and bring to a boil over high heat. Once at a boil, add a pinch of salt and the pasta and cook until the pasta is al dente, following the package directions. Drain well.

2. Put the cooked pasta, feta, ham, olives, tomatoes, cucumbers, and bell peppers in a medium-sized mixing bowl.

3. Add the dressing and toss until the ingredients are evenly coated. Season to taste with salt and pepper. Divide between two serving bowls. Best served fresh, while the pasta is still slightly warm, but can last in the fridge for up to 4 days.

ALLERGENS

NOTE: To make this dish gluten-free, use a gluten-free pasta.

GRAPEFRUIT DELIGHT SALAD

  YIELD: 1 serving **PREP TIME:** 10 minutes

Grapefruit is one of my favorite fruits to eat during the winter and early spring. I usually eat it with a bunch of sugar spooned on top. However, the segments are also great in a green salad, and the juice makes an excellent dressing! Crushed red pepper may sound odd in a salad dressing, but it's a great partner for the honey.

SALAD

3 cups spring mix

¼ cup chopped raw walnuts

¼ cup crumbled feta cheese

¼ cup chopped grapefruit segments

DRESSING

3 tablespoons extra-virgin olive oil

3 tablespoons grapefruit juice

1 tablespoon honey

¼ teaspoon crushed red pepper

½ teaspoon minced garlic

Pinch of salt

Pinch of ground black pepper

1. Place the spring mix, walnuts, feta, and grapefruit segments in a serving bowl.

2. In a separate small bowl, whisk together the ingredients for the dressing until well combined.

3. Pour the dressing over the salad, then toss and enjoy.

ALLERGENS

VEGETARIAN'S DELIGHT

OPTION

YIELD: 1 serving   **PREP TIME:** 5 minutes   **COOK TIME:** 6 minutes

In my humble opinion, vegetarians know how to make excellent sandwiches. One of my close friends from my hometown, who is a vegetarian, inspired this recipe. One day she made me a sandwich with hummus and a perfectly roasted red pepper, and I thank her all the time for turning me on to the combination. I hope you like it too! *Note:* You can simply toast the bread in a toaster oven or toaster and then assemble the sandwich, or, if you don't own either of those appliances but do have an air fryer, you can assemble the sandwich and air-fry it till toasty brown.

2 slices whole wheat bread

2 tablespoons garlic hummus, plus more if desired

2 slices Gouda cheese

¼ cup arugula

3 slices cucumber

½ cup roasted red peppers, sliced

1 slice red onion

Pinch of salt

Pinch of ground black pepper

Pinch of dried parsley

To assemble the sandwich with toasted bread, toast the bread in a toaster oven or toaster. Smear the hummus on one of the bread slices, then top with the cheese, arugula, cucumber, roasted red peppers, onion, salt, pepper, and parsley. Set the other slice of bread on top and enjoy.

To assemble the sandwich with untoasted bread using an air fryer, smear the hummus on one of the bread slices, then top with the cheese, arugula, cucumber, roasted red peppers, onion, salt, pepper, and parsley. Set the other slice of bread on top. Place the sandwich in the air-fryer basket and air-fry at 375°F for 6 minutes, or until the bread is toasted. Flip the sandwich over halfway through toasting. Remove and enjoy.

ALLERGENS

NOTE: To make this sandwich gluten-free, use gluten-free bread.

CHEESY CHICKEN ENCHILADA WRAP

OPTION

YIELD: 1 serving   **PREP TIME:** 10 minutes (not including time to cook chicken)
COOK TIME: 45 seconds

A cheesy enchilada is one of my favorite Mexican meals. But how does one turn it into a fast, portable lunch? That was the goal of this recipe, and I think I achieved it. The trick is drizzling the enchilada sauce over the melty chicken and cheese filling, topping it with beans and veggies, and rolling the whole thing up into a wrap. Take it to go! No knife and fork needed.

1 (10-inch) whole wheat flour tortilla

⅔ cup shredded cooked chicken breast

½ cup shredded Colby cheese

3 tablespoons enchilada sauce

1 tablespoon chopped fresh cilantro, or 1 teaspoon dried cilantro

1 teaspoon dried parsley

½ teaspoon garlic powder

Pinch of salt

Pinch of ground black pepper

½ cup chopped lettuce

½ cup diced tomatoes

¼ cup canned black beans, rinsed and drained

¼ cup sliced yellow onions

1. Place the tortilla on a microwave-safe plate and layer the shredded chicken and cheese on the bottom third of the tortilla. Microwave on medium-high just until the tortilla is warmed and the cheese is beginning to melt, about 45 seconds.

2. Top the chicken and cheese with the enchilada sauce, cilantro, parsley, garlic powder, salt, and pepper. Then layer on the lettuce, tomatoes, black beans, and onions.

3. Roll up the tortilla burrito-style, tucking in the bottom and sides and then rolling from bottom to top. Enjoy on the go!

ALLERGENS

NOTE: To make this wrap gluten-free, use a gluten-free tortilla.

BUFFALO CHICKEN SALAD SANDWICH

OPTION

YIELD: 1 serving   **PREP TIME:** 10 minutes (not including time to cook chicken)

This recipe takes your classic chicken salad sandwich and kicks it up a notch. I am all for tradition, but sometimes it's nice to switch it up. I like to make it with extra Buffalo sauce because I like spicy food, but feel free to decrease the amount to your spice tolerance level.

BUFFALO CHICKEN SALAD

¾ cup shredded cooked chicken breast

¼ cup diced celery

¼ cup diced red onions

2 tablespoons Buffalo sauce

2 tablespoons ranch dressing

½ teaspoon garlic powder

2 slices whole wheat bread, toasted

1 cup torn lettuce

¼ cup crumbled blue cheese

1. In a medium-sized mixing bowl, mix the shredded chicken, celery, onions, Buffalo sauce, ranch dressing, and garlic powder until well combined.

2. To assemble the sandwich, spread the chicken salad on a slice of toasted bread, then top with the lettuce, blue cheese, and second slice of bread. Cut in half and enjoy.

ALLERGENS

NOTE: To make this sandwich gluten-free, use gluten-free bread.

SWEET 'N' SALTY TURKEY MELT

OPTION

YIELD: 1 serving   **PREP TIME:** 8 minutes   **COOK TIME:** 10 minutes

Sometimes I crave something that is both sweet and salty. Here is a recipe for those of you who have the same types of cravings. In this sandwich, the sweetness of the fig jam complements the savory turkey perfectly, and the Brie brings a creaminess that further binds the flavors together. I hope you enjoy it as much as I do!

2 slices whole wheat bread

3 slices Brie cheese

¼ cup arugula

4 slices deli turkey

1½ tablespoons raw walnuts

1 tablespoon fig jam

Pinch of salt

Pinch of ground black pepper

1. Preheat a medium-sized frying pan over medium-high heat.

2. On one slice of bread, layer the Brie, arugula, turkey, and walnuts. Smear the fig jam on the second slice of bread and sprinkle the jam with the salt and pepper. Top the sandwich fillings with the second slice of bread, jam side down.

3. Coat one side of the sandwich with cooking oil spray and place it in the frying pan, oiled side down.

4. Once toasted on the underside, spray the top piece of bread and flip the sandwich over. Cook until toasted on both sides and the cheese is slightly melted. Remove, cut in half, and enjoy.

ALLERGENS

NOTE: To make this sandwich gluten-free, use gluten-free bread.

THE ULTIMATE GRILLED CHEESE

OPTION   OPTION

YIELD: 1 serving   **PREP TIME:** 10 minutes   **COOK TIME:** 6 to 9 minutes, depending on method

Grilled cheese is an obvious go-to when it comes to quick and easy lunches. Sometimes I get bored with the basic version and feel the need to step it up a little. Loading it up with veggies is one way to add not only fiber and vitamins but also depth of flavor. If you don't have an air fryer, you can use a frying pan.

2 slices whole wheat bread

2 slices cheddar cheese

2 tablespoons grated Parmesan cheese

1 slice part-skim mozzarella cheese

½ small avocado, sliced

2 slices medium tomato

¼ cup fresh spinach

Pinch of salt

Pinch of ground black pepper

Pinch of garlic powder

Pinch of dried parsley

2 tablespoons olive oil (for stovetop), or cooking oil spray (for air fryer)

1. *If using a hot plate or the stovetop,* preheat a medium-sized frying pan over medium-high heat.

2. On one slice of bread, layer the cheddar, Parmesan, and mozzarella cheeses, then the avocado, tomato, and spinach. Season with the salt, pepper, garlic powder, and parsley. Top with the second slice of bread.

3. *To cook the sandwich in an air fryer,* spray both sides of the sandwich with cooking oil spray and place in the air-fryer basket. Air-fry at 375°F for 5 minutes, or until golden brown. Take out, flip the sandwich over, and continue to air-fry until golden brown on both sides, another 4 minutes.

4. *To cook the sandwich on a hot plate or the stovetop,* pour the olive oil into the preheated pan and fry one side of the sandwich until toasted and golden brown, 3 to 4 minutes. Flip the sandwich over to toast the other side, another 3 to 4 minutes.

5. Cut the sandwich in half and enjoy.

ALLERGENS

NOTE: To make this sandwich vegetarian, use a Parmesan cheese made without animal rennet. To make it gluten-free, use gluten-free bread.

TURKEY SALAD SANDWICH WITH DRIED CHERRIES

OPTION

YIELD: 1 serving   **PREP TIME:** 10 minutes (not including time to cook turkey)

I created this simple combination by chance on the day after Thanksgiving. All we had left over was a whole lot of turkey—no cranberry sauce or even dried cranberries—so I made a turkey salad sandwich with dried cherries instead. Their sweetness works perfectly with the savoriness of the turkey. If you don't have turkey on hand, you could always make this recipe with rotisserie chicken, a convenient cheat that's equally good.

TURKEY SALAD

½ cup shredded cooked turkey (white and/or dark meat)

3 tablespoons mayonnaise

3 tablespoons diced celery

1 tablespoon finely diced red onions

2 tablespoons sweetened dried cherries

1 tablespoon dried parsley

Pinch of garlic powder

Pinch of salt

Pinch of ground black pepper

2 slices whole wheat bread, toasted

2 slices medium tomato

¼ cup spring mix

1. Put the turkey, mayonnaise, celery, onions, dried cherries, parsley, garlic powder, salt, and pepper in a small mixing bowl. Mix until the ingredients are evenly distributed.

2. Spread the turkey salad on one piece of toast and top with the tomato slices and spring mix. Place the second piece of toast on top, cut the sandwich in half, and enjoy.

ALLERGENS

OPTION

NOTE: To make this sandwich gluten-free, use gluten-free bread. To make it egg-free, use vegan mayo.

THE "I DON'T HAVE TIME TO MAKE A SANDWICH" SANDWICH

OPTION

YIELD: 1 serving   **PREP TIME:** 5 minutes

This may be a paradox, because if you do not have time to make a sandwich, then you just do not make a sandwich. However, the ingredients listed here do not need to be prepped in any particular way. All you need to do is grab them from the fridge and layer everything to your liking.

2 slices whole wheat bread, toasted

1 tablespoon pesto

2 slices cheddar cheese

¼ cup sprouts (such as alfalfa, clover, or radish)

2 slices deli turkey

2 slices salami

Pinch of garlic powder

Pinch of ground black pepper

1. Smear one side of each piece of toast with the pesto, dividing it equally between them. On one piece of toast, layer the cheese, sprouts, turkey, and salami. Season with the garlic powder and pepper.

2. Top with the second piece of toast, slice in half, and enjoy!

ALLERGENS

NOTE: To make this sandwich gluten-free, use gluten-free bread.

ELVIS'S FAVORITE SANDWICH

OPTION

YIELD: 1 serving   **PREP TIME:** 5 minutes   **COOK TIME:** 8 to 16 minutes, depending on method

Obviously, this recipe is inspired by the King's favorite lunch, which was a fried peanut butter, banana, and bacon sandwich. I tweaked it a little bit by air-frying the banana with cinnamon and sugar and using turkey bacon to add a lean protein. If only Elvis were alive to try this version!

1 banana, cut into ½-inch rounds

1 slice turkey bacon

½ teaspoon ground cinnamon

Pinch of granulated sugar

Pinch of salt

1½ tablespoons strawberry jam

2 slices white or whole wheat bread, toasted

2 tablespoons natural peanut butter

1. *If using the toaster oven or oven,* preheat it to 400°F and line a small sheet pan with parchment paper. *If using an air fryer,* line the air-fryer basked with parchment paper.

2. Place the banana and bacon in the prepared air-fryer basket or sheet pan. Lightly coat the banana with cooking oil spray and season with the cinnamon, sugar, and salt.

3. Air-fry at 365°F for 5 minutes or bake in the oven for 6 to 8 minutes, until the banana is slightly caramelized. Remove the banana and set aside. Air-fry the bacon for another 3 minutes or bake the bacon for another 6 to 8 minutes, until crispy.

4. Cut the bacon crosswise into thirds.

5. Smear the jam on one piece of toast and smear the peanut butter on the other piece. Place the bacon and banana on top of the jam, then top with the peanut butter–smeared toast and enjoy.

ALLERGENS

NOTE: To make this sandwich gluten-free, use gluten-free bread.

MASHED CHICKPEA FLATBREAD

OPTION

YIELD: 1 serving   **PREP TIME:** 10 minutes

During my first year working as a dietitian, flatbread spread with mashed chickpeas was my favorite lunch. It is simple to make, easy to transport, and keeps you full for hours due to the high fiber content. You don't even need to cook anything, which is another huge upside to this simple recipe. You might think of it as a modern twist on the open-faced sandwich, but one that is much easier to eat—no knife and fork required!

½ cup canned chickpeas, rinsed and drained

2 tablespoons mayonnaise

1 teaspoon Dijon mustard

1 teaspoon lemon juice

½ teaspoon dried parsley

½ teaspoon garlic powder

Pinch of salt

Pinch of ground black pepper

3 lettuce leaves

1 small tomato, sliced

1 (10-inch) flatbread, toasted

1 tablespoon chopped fresh cilantro, for garnish

1. In a medium-sized mixing bowl, mash the chickpeas until more than half of them are broken down.

2. Add the mayonnaise, mustard, lemon juice, parsley, garlic powder, salt, and pepper and stir until well combined.

3. Layer the lettuce leaves and tomato slices on the toasted flatbread. Top with the chickpea mixture and cilantro and enjoy!

ALLERGENS

OPTION

NOTE: To make this "sandwich" gluten-free, use gluten-free flatbread. To make it egg-free, use vegan mayo.

chapter 3:
SATISFYING SNACKIES

Hungry, but not hungry enough for a meal? Then it's time for a hearty snack! This chapter is filled with delicious recipes that are easy to prepare, require minimal ingredients, and provide real staying power, holding you over until your next meal. Many of these snacks would work equally well as appetizers for your next dinner party; simply double or triple the recipe as needed.

ROASTED TOMATO & FETA CHEESE DIP

  YIELD: 3 servings   **PREP TIME:** 5 minutes   **COOK TIME:** 40 minutes

Nothing is better than a warm, savory dip that's simple to make, which is why this is one of my go-to recipes when I need a cozy yet not-too-heavy savory snack. It is rich in protein and heart-healthy monounsaturated fats and full of flavor. I like to eat it with whole wheat toast, but it also pairs well with crackers.

⅔ cup cherry tomatoes

¼ cup crumbled feta cheese

¼ cup olive oil

1 teaspoon dried parsley

½ teaspoon crushed red pepper

Pinch of salt

Pinch of ground black pepper

1. Preheat the toaster oven or oven to 325°F.

2. In a 2-quart baking dish, gently toss the tomatoes and feta in the olive oil until evenly coated. Sprinkle with the parsley, crushed red pepper, salt, and black pepper.

3. Bake for 30 to 40 minutes, until the oil is bubbling around the edges. Serve hot.

4. Leftover dip can last in the fridge for up to 5 days. To reheat, microwave on high for 1 minute.

ALLERGENS

PEPPERONI PIZZA STICKS

OPTION

YIELD: 2 servings   **PREP TIME:** 5 minutes   **COOK TIME:** 8 to 13 minutes, depending on method

This is the lazy way to make cheesy pepperoni-filled pizza sticks. And because it takes just a few minutes to whip these up, this recipe is perfect for when you're short on energy or time but still want a filling snack. You can make it in either an air fryer or the oven. Pair these sticks with your favorite marinara sauce.

4 part-skim mozzarella cheese sticks

12 pepperoni slices

2 (10-inch) whole wheat flour tortillas, halved

½ teaspoon Italian seasoning

1 tablespoon grated Parmesan cheese, for garnish

Marinara sauce, for dipping

1. *If using the toaster oven or oven,* preheat it to 375°F and line a small sheet pan with aluminum foil. *If using an air fryer,* line the air-fryer basket with foil.

2. Place 1 cheese stick and 3 pepperoni slices on each tortilla half, along the cut edge. Starting at the cut edge, roll up each tortilla half from end to end, forming a tube.

3. Lightly coat each pizza stick with cooking oil spray and sprinkle with the Italian seasoning.

4. Set the pizza sticks seam side down on the prepared pan or basket. Air-fry at 350°F for 8 minutes or bake in the oven for 10 to 13 minutes, until slightly golden brown.

5. Dust the Parmesan cheese over the sticks and enjoy with marinara sauce. Best served fresh but can last in the fridge for up to 3 days. To reheat, microwave on high for 45 seconds.

ALLERGENS

NOTE: To make these sticks gluten-free, use gluten-free tortillas.

AIR FRYER PARMESAN GARLIC CARROT FRIES

 YIELD: 2 servings   **PREP TIME:** 10 minutes   **COOK TIME:** 15 minutes

Who would have thought that carrots make excellent fries? Not me! Then I experimented with this method and learned the truth. If you have a few extra carrots on hand, I highly recommend you try this delicious recipe. The garlic and Parmesan flavors pair perfectly with the slight sweetness of the carrots. Don't knock it until you try it! (If you don't already own an air fryer, this is one of those recipes that makes it worth investing in one; these fries just aren't as good made any other way.)

3 large carrots

1 tablespoon olive oil

3 tablespoons grated Parmesan cheese

½ teaspoon garlic powder

Pinch of salt

Pinch of ground black pepper

Ranch dressing, for serving (optional)

1. Trim and peel the carrots, then cut them in half crosswise if extra-long. Next, cut them lengthwise into french fry–like strips about ⅓ inch wide.

2. Put the carrot strips in a medium-sized bowl and toss with the olive oil, Parmesan cheese, garlic powder, salt, and pepper until evenly coated.

3. Line the air-fryer basket with parchment paper. Spread the seasoned carrot strips in a single layer in the prepared basket and air-fry at 400°F for 15 minutes, or until fork-tender and beginning to brown.

4. Serve with ranch dressing on the side, if desired. The fries are best eaten immediately but can last in the fridge for up to 3 days. To reheat, air-fry at 375°F for about 2 minutes or bake in a preheated 400°F oven for about 5 minutes.

ALLERGENS

SWEET POTATO CHIPS

 YIELD: 1 serving **PREP TIME:** 10 minutes, plus 20 minutes to soak sweet potatoes
COOK TIME: 15 to 30 minutes, depending on method

Eating sweet potatoes is one of the best ways to meet your daily fiber and vitamin A needs. Not only are they rich in nutrients, but they are sweet, tasty, and versatile. This recipe is one of my favorite savory treatments of sweet potatoes, and the chips stay crisp for a while. Sometimes I make a double batch to have extras for the week. They make a great lunch box addition or on-the-go snack, and they'll keep in an airtight container in the pantry for up to a week. You can make them in the oven or in an air fryer.

1 medium sweet potato, scrubbed

2 tablespoons olive oil

½ teaspoon garlic powder

½ teaspoon onion powder

Pinch of salt

Pinch of ground black pepper

Sliced green onions, for garnish (optional)

1. *If using the toaster oven or oven,* preheat it to 375°F and line a small sheet pan with parchment paper. *If using an air fryer,* line the air-fryer basket with parchment paper.

2. Slice the sweet potato into thin rounds, not more than ⅛ inch thick. Put the slices in a medium-sized bowl, cover with cold water, and soak for 20 minutes. Drain and pat dry.

3. Dry the bowl well, then return the sweet potato slices to it. Add the olive oil, garlic powder, onion powder, salt, and pepper and toss until the slices are evenly coated.

4. Spread the seasoned sweet potato slices in a single layer in the prepared pan or basket.

5. *If using an air fryer,* air-fry at 365°F for 10 minutes, then remove the basket from the air fryer and stir the chips. Increase the temperature to 400°F and air-fry for another 5 minutes, or until the chips are crispy.

If using the oven, bake for 25 to 30 minutes, until crispy, flipping the chips over halfway through cooking.

6. Serve garnished with sliced green onions, if desired.

AIR FRYER BBQ POTATO SKIN SNACKERS

  YIELD: 1 serving   **PREP TIME:** 10 minutes   **COOK TIME:** 7 minutes

Potatoes and BBQ flavor go hand in hand, like chocolate and peanut butter. Using just the skins of the potatoes may seem unconventional, but it's an excellent way to reduce food waste. So, the next time you are peeling potatoes, don't throw away the skins. Make this recipe instead!

2 large russet potatoes (about 1 pound)

1 tablespoon olive oil

½ teaspoon brown sugar

½ teaspoon smoked paprika

½ teaspoon garlic powder

Pinch of ground mustard

Pinch of salt

Pinch of ground black pepper

Chopped fresh parsley, for garnish (optional)

1. Scrub the potatoes, then peel them with a potato peeler. Put the skins in a medium-sized bowl. Save the peeled potatoes for another use.

2. To the bowl with the potato skins, add the olive oil, brown sugar, smoked paprika, garlic powder, ground mustard, salt, and pepper. Mix until the potato skins are evenly coated.

3. Line the air-fryer basket with parchment paper. Spread the seasoned potato skins in a single layer in the prepared basket and air-fry at 375°F for 7 minutes, or until crispy. Garnish with parsley, if desired.

SLOW COOKER CHICKEN ENCHILADA DIP

 YIELD: 4 servings   **PREP TIME:** 12 minutes   **COOK TIME:** 2 or 3½ hours

A slow cooker is one of the best appliances to use for making dips—especially this chicken enchilada dip. It is packed with flavor and easy to make, which makes it perfect for dinner parties or pitch-in lunches at work. Pair it with your favorite tortilla chips.

1 boneless, skinless chicken breast (about 6 ounces)

½ cup chicken broth

1 (8-ounce) package ⅓-less-fat cream cheese (aka Neufchâtel)

½ cup shredded cheddar cheese

½ cup shredded part-skim mozzarella cheese

⅓ cup diced red onions

1 tablespoon dried cilantro leaves

1 teaspoon garlic powder

1 (14½-ounce) can diced tomatoes, drained

½ cup canned black beans, rinsed and drained

½ teaspoon ground black pepper

Chopped fresh cilantro, for garnish (optional)

1. Put the chicken breast, broth, cream cheese, cheddar, mozzarella, onions, dried cilantro, and garlic powder in a slow cooker and cook for 1½ hours on high or 3 hours on low, or until the chicken is fully cooked (the thickest part of the breast should reach 165°F).

2. Remove the chicken from the slow cooker and use two forks to shred it. Return it to the slow cooker and add the tomatoes and black beans. Stir until well combined, then cook on high for another 30 minutes.

3. Transfer the dip to a serving dish and garnish with fresh cilantro, if desired. Serve immediately. Store leftovers in the fridge for up to 4 days. To reheat, microwave on high for 1 minute 30 seconds.

ALLERGENS

2-INGREDIENT PEPPERONI CHEESE BITES

 YIELD: 2 servings   **PREP TIME:** 2 minutes, plus 30 minutes to cool
COOK TIME: 20 minutes

These savory bites are perfect when you want something warm and savory to eat and want to exert minimal effort to make it. The next time you are up late and looking for a snack, make this recipe instead of eating shredded cheese from the bag!

⅓ **cup shredded part-skim mozzarella cheese**

8 slices pepperoni

½ **teaspoon dried oregano leaves (optional)**

1. Preheat the toaster oven or oven to 400°F and line a small sheet pan with parchment paper.

2. Spoon 1 mounded tablespoon of cheese onto the prepared pan. Repeat 7 more times, making sure there are 2 inches of space between piles of cheese. Top each pile with a slice of pepperoni.

3. Bake for 15 to 20 minutes, or until the edges of the cheese bites start to brown. Allow to cool for 30 minutes before serving. These are best served fresh, but if you have leftovers, they can last in the fridge for up to 4 days. They're great cold, straight from the fridge.

ALLERGENS

VEGGIE & RICOTTA-STUFFED PORTABELLA MUSHROOMS

  YIELD: 4 servings   **PREP TIME:** 10 minutes   **COOK TIME:** 25 minutes

Portabella mushroom caps are the perfect base for just about anything, but they're especially good when stuffed with veggies and ricotta. This nourishing recipe has a perfect balance of protein, fat, and fiber. Enjoy one of these caps as a serious snack, eat two for a satisfying lunch, or offer them as an appetizer when you have company.

4 (2-inch) portabella mushroom caps

3 tablespoons olive oil, divided

¼ teaspoon garlic powder

Salt and pepper

½ cup frozen bell peppers and onions medley

¼ cup cherry tomatoes

1 teaspoon Italian seasoning

½ teaspoon garlic salt

RICOTTA FILLING

½ cup ricotta cheese

1 teaspoon Italian seasoning

1 teaspoon dried parsley

½ teaspoon garlic powder

Pinch of salt

Pinch of ground black pepper

ALLERGENS

1. Preheat the toaster oven or oven to 375°F and line a small sheet pan with parchment paper.

2. Put the mushroom caps in a medium-sized bowl and drizzle evenly with 2 tablespoons of the olive oil. Sprinkle the caps with the garlic powder and a pinch each of salt and pepper and mix gently to distribute the oil and seasonings on both sides of the mushrooms. Place on the prepared pan, cavity side up.

3. Defrost the frozen peppers and onions in the microwave, then drain and put in a medium-sized mixing bowl. Add the tomatoes to the defrosted vegetables. Drizzle the vegetables with the remaining tablespoon of olive oil, then sprinkle on the Italian seasoning, garlic salt, and a pinch of pepper. Stir until the vegetables are evenly coated, then spread them on the pan next to the mushroom caps.

4. Bake the mushroom caps and vegetables for 15 to 20 minutes, until slightly roasted.

5. Meanwhile, make the ricotta filling: Mix the ricotta, Italian seasoning, parsley, garlic powder, salt, and pepper in a small bowl until well combined.

6. Remove the pan from the oven and set the mushrooms and vegetables aside to cool for 10 minutes.

7. Fill the mushroom caps with the ricotta mixture, dividing it evenly among them, then top with the vegetables. Serve immediately. Store leftovers in the fridge for up to 2 days. To reheat, microwave on high for 1 minute.

ROASTED TOMATO & HERBED RICOTTA TOAST

OPTION

YIELD: 1 serving   **PREP TIME:** 5 minutes   **COOK TIME:** 20 minutes

Roasted tomatoes and herbed ricotta are a match made in heaven. All thanks to Italians for creating such a divine flavor combination, which is like the Ross and Rachel of food pairings. The beauty of this recipe is its simplicity: when you top toast with tomatoes and ricotta, you get a light yet satisfying snack (or light meal) that is nutrient-dense and nourishing.

3 thick slices medium tomato

1 tablespoon olive oil

1 tablespoon dried basil, plus more for garnish (optional)

⅓ cup ricotta cheese

1 teaspoon dried parsley

¼ teaspoon garlic powder

Pinch of salt

Pinch of ground black pepper

1 large slice whole wheat bread, toasted

1. Preheat the toaster oven or oven to 400°F.

2. Put the tomato slices in a small baking dish, then drizzle with the olive oil and sprinkle with the basil. Bake until the tomatoes have shriveled slightly, 15 to 20 minutes.

3. When the tomatoes are nearly done baking, mix together the ricotta, parsley, garlic powder, salt, and pepper until well combined.

4. Spread the ricotta mixture on the toast, then top with the roasted tomatoes. Drizzle the remaining oil and tomato juice in the baking dish over the toast and garnish with basil, if desired. Enjoy!

ALLERGENS

NOTE: To make this toast gluten-free, use gluten-free bread.

BAKED JALAPEÑO, RASPBERRY & CREAM CHEESE DIP

  YIELD: 4 servings   **PREP TIME:** 5 minutes   **COOK TIME:** 20 minutes

This is my mother's go-to appetizer when she has people over for a dinner party. It always gets devoured instantly—mostly by me. It hits all the creamy, savory, sweet, and spicy flavors in one bite. With only three ingredients, this dip is super easy to make. But beware—it is addictive!

1 (8-ounce) package ⅓-less-fat cream cheese (aka Neufchâtel)

⅔ cup raspberry jam

1 jalapeño pepper, finely diced

Crackers and/or pretzels, for serving

1. Preheat the toaster oven or oven to 350°F.

2. Place the cream cheese in the center of a 2-quart baking dish. Spoon the raspberry jam on top of the cream cheese and sprinkle with the diced jalapeño.

3. Bake for 15 to 20 minutes, until the cream cheese is gooey.

4. Enjoy hot with crackers or pretzels. The dip can last in the fridge for up to 5 days. To reheat, microwave on high for 40 seconds.

NOTES: If you like less heat, remove the seeds from the jalapeno pepper.

To make this snack gluten-free, serve the dip with gluten-free crackers or pretzels.

ALLERGENS

SLOW COOKER SPINACH ARTICHOKE DIP

  YIELD: 2 servings   **PREP TIME:** 10 minutes   **COOK TIME:** 1 hour 20 minutes

Warm spinach artichoke dip is a classic at family functions, potlucks, and holiday gatherings. It is creamy, savory, and full of deliciousness! Not many people say they do not like this dip, and that's why you can find so many variations of it on the internet. So, here is my tasty but simplified and compact version of the beloved dip.

2 cups fresh spinach

1 (14-ounce) can quartered artichoke hearts, drained

4 ounces ⅓-less-fat cream cheese (aka Neufchâtel) (½ cup)

½ cup shredded part-skim mozzarella cheese

½ cup chicken broth

1 teaspoon minced garlic

1 teaspoon grated lemon zest

½ teaspoon onion powder

½ teaspoon ground black pepper

¼ teaspoon salt

Tortilla chips or other scoopers of choice, for serving

1. Put all of the ingredients in a slow cooker and cook on low for 1 hour 20 minutes, stirring every 20 minutes. The dip is ready when the spinach has wilted, the cheese has melted, and everything is heated through and evenly combined.

2. Serve hot with tortilla chips or other scoopers. The dip will last in the refrigerator for up to 5 days. To reheat, microwave on high for 30 seconds.

ALLERGENS

chapter 4:
EASY-PEASY DINNERS

Congrats! You made it to dinnertime! Let's unwind and make some nourishing and comforting meals without exerting any more effort than we need to. This chapter is full of the go-to dinners that I make when I am feeling low on energy, am under the weather, or just want something simple. I hope you enjoy them and find them as helpful as I do.

In this chapter, you'll find two sections of recipes: "Dinners in a Dash" and "Slow and Steady Suppers." The great majority of the dinners in the first group can be prepared in half an hour or less; none takes longer than an hour. The "Slow and Steady" recipes are all made in a slow cooker and range from satisfying soups to chicken Parm and pot roast. I love to tuck into a comforting bowl of soup at the end of the day, but of course all the soups in this chapter make great lunch options the next day.

POLENTA PIE

 YIELD: 3 servings   **PREP TIME:** 8 minutes   **COOK TIME:** 20 minutes

This savory pie has been a family favorite for years; it's my mother's go-to recipe on days when time is crunched and she wants something super easy to make. Not only is this pie simple to prepare, but it is nutritionally balanced and filling. I like using spinach, ham, American cheese, and tomato, but you can improvise with other veggies and proteins.

5 cups water

3 tablespoons olive oil

Salt

1½ cups uncooked polenta

⅔ cup fresh spinach

½ cup chopped deli ham

4 slices American cheese

1 medium tomato, sliced

1 teaspoon ground dried oregano

1 teaspoon dried parsley

Pinch of ground black pepper

FOR GARNISH (optional)

Finely chopped fresh parsley

Crushed red pepper

1. Preheat the toaster oven or oven to 350°F. Grease a 6-inch deep pie dish or a 1-quart baking dish with cooking oil spray.

2. Put the water, olive oil, and a pinch of salt in a large microwave-safe bowl, cover with a microwave-safe plate, and microwave on high for 5 minutes, or until the water is boiling.

3. Add the polenta to the boiling water, stir, cover the bowl with the plate again, and microwave on high for 1 minute. Then let the polenta sit for 5 minutes, or until it has absorbed all the water.

4. Put half of the cooked polenta in the prepared pie dish, spreading it evenly across the bottom. Top evenly with the spinach, ham, and cheese. Spread the rest of the polenta across the top, then add the tomato slices. Sprinkle with the oregano, parsley, black pepper, and another pinch of salt.

5. Bake for 10 to 15 minutes, until lightly browned on the edges. Top with some fresh parsley and crushed red pepper, if desired, and enjoy! Best served fresh but can last in the fridge for up to 5 days. To reheat, microwave on high for 1 minute.

ALLERGENS

MICROWAVE BUFFALO CHICKEN MAC & CHEESE

OPTION

YIELD: 1 serving   **PREP TIME:** 10 minutes (not including time to cook chicken)
COOK TIME: 10 minutes

If you are a college student living in a dorm, then you will appreciate this meal. When I was a freshman, this recipe was a favorite late-night meal of mine. I did not have a stovetop to boil water and cook pasta, so I figured out how to cook pasta in the microwave. Thankfully, it was a success!

¾ cup macaroni or other small pasta of choice

1½ cups water

Salt

¼ cup shredded part-skim mozzarella cheese

¼ cup shredded sharp cheddar cheese

1 tablespoon pasta water (from above)

1½ teaspoons milk of choice

1½ teaspoons unsalted butter

Pinch of ground black pepper

¼ cup shredded cooked chicken breast

1 tablespoon Buffalo sauce

Sliced green onions, for garnish (optional)

1. Put the pasta, water, and a pinch of salt in a medium-sized microwave-safe bowl. Microwave uncovered on medium-high for 5 minutes. Take out and stir, then microwave again for another 5 minutes, or until the pasta is al dente.

2. Reserve 1 tablespoon of the pasta cooking water, then drain the pasta and return it to the bowl.

3. To the bowl with the pasta, add the mozzarella and cheddar cheeses, reserved pasta water, milk, butter, pepper, and another pinch of salt. Mix until the ingredients are well combined and the cheese is gooey. If the cheese is not gooey, microwave for 40 seconds.

4. Fold in the shredded chicken and Buffalo sauce. Garnish with sliced green onions before serving, if desired.

ALLERGENS

NOTE: To make this dish gluten-free, use a gluten-free pasta.

AIR FRYER CRAB CAKES

OPTION

YIELD: 3 servings   **PREP TIME:** 10 minutes   **COOK TIME:** 11 minutes

Who doesn't love a good crab cake—especially a slightly spicy one that takes minimal effort to make? If you don't like heat, however, feel free to omit the Sriracha sauce. This recipe is another one that my mom inspired. Crab cakes are her favorite meal. I made this version for her once, and now she requests it for her birthday every year. Instead of pan-frying the crab cakes—the conventional way to cook them—I use the air fryer to make the cooking process easier.

1 (8-ounce) package imitation crab (flake style)

½ cup mayonnaise

1 large egg

1 teaspoon lemon juice

1 teaspoon Sriracha sauce

1 cup plain breadcrumbs

3 tablespoons chopped fresh parsley

1 tablespoon dried minced onions

½ teaspoon garlic powder

½ teaspoon Old Bay seasoning

Pinch of salt

Pinch of ground black pepper

FOR GARNISH/SERVING (optional)

Lemon slices

Sliced green onions

1. Put the imitation crab in a medium-sized bowl and use two forks to shred it into smaller pieces. Add the rest of the ingredients for the crab cakes and mix until well combined.

2. Line the air-fryer basket with parchment paper or aluminum foil. Using a ¼-cup measuring cup, scoop the mixture into nine equal portions, then use your hands to form them into 1-inch-thick rounds. Place in the prepared basket and air-fry at 390°F for 11 minutes, or until the cakes are golden brown.

3. Serve hot with lemon slices and garnished with sliced green onions, if desired. Best served fresh but can last in the fridge for up to 4 days. To reheat, microwave on high for 1 minute.

ALLERGENS

NOTE: To make these crab cakes gluten-free, use gluten-free breadcrumbs.

CHICKEN & POTATO GOULASH

 YIELD: 1 serving   **PREP TIME:** 10 minutes   **COOK TIME:** 22 to 34 minutes, depending on method

Chicken, potatoes, and cheese—a match made in heaven. This recipe is perfect not just for dinner, but also for breakfast or lunch, and it's even better as leftovers the next day. It can be cooked in an air fryer or in the oven. I like to use the air fryer because it makes the potatoes crispy all over. However, if you prefer to use the oven, it will still come out great!

1 medium russet potato (about 8 ounces), scrubbed

1 boneless, skinless chicken breast (about 6 ounces)

3 tablespoons olive oil, divided

½ teaspoon garlic powder, divided

½ teaspoon onion powder, divided

½ teaspoon smoked paprika, divided

¼ teaspoon salt, divided

¼ teaspoon ground black pepper, divided

¼ cup shredded cheddar cheese

Sliced fresh or dried chives, for garnish

1. *If using an air fryer,* line the air-fryer basket with aluminum foil. *If using the toaster oven or oven,* preheat it to 375°F and line a small sheet pan with foil.

2. Cut the potato into ¼-inch dice. Then cut the chicken into ¾-inch cubes. Set the chicken aside.

3. Put the diced potato in a medium-sized mixing bowl. Drizzle with 2 tablespoons of the olive oil and add half of the garlic powder, onion powder, smoked paprika, salt, and pepper. Mix until the potato pieces are evenly coated.

4. Spread the seasoned potatoes in the prepared basket or pan. Air-fry at 375°F for 10 minutes or bake in the oven for 20 minutes, or until fork-tender.

5. Meanwhile, put the cubed chicken in a medium-sized mixing bowl. Drizzle with the remaining tablespoon of olive oil and add the remaining garlic powder, onion powder, smoked paprika, salt, and pepper. Mix until the chicken is evenly coated in the oil and seasonings. Set aside until the potatoes are done cooking.

6. Once the potatoes are done, remove them to a plate and spread the chicken in the same basket or pan. Air-fry at 320°F for 12 minutes or bake in the oven (still at 375°F) for 10 to 12 minutes, until the chicken is thoroughly cooked.

7. Return the potatoes to the basket or pan and mix with the chicken. Sprinkle the cheese over them and air-fry at 350°F or bake in the oven for 2 minutes, or until the cheese has melted.

8. Sprinkle some chives over the goulash and enjoy!

ALLERGENS

PIZZA QUESADILLA

OPTION

YIELD: 1 serving   **PREP TIME:** 5 minutes   **COOK TIME:** 15 minutes

If you like both pizza and quesadillas, then you will appreciate this recipe. It combines the flavors of pizza with the quesadilla-making technique. My favorite part is when you cut into it and take that first slice—there is that beautiful cheese pull. I ate this for lunch and dinner a lot during my dietetic internship and graduate school days because it is so simple to make and so satisfying. If you are a busy bee, I hope this recipe helps you too!

3 tablespoons marinara sauce

2 (10-inch) whole wheat flour tortillas

½ cup shredded part-skim mozzarella cheese

½ teaspoon dried minced onions

Pinch of Italian seasoning

5 slices pepperoni

Sliced green onions, for garnish (optional)

1. Preheat the toaster oven or oven to 400°F. Line a small sheet pan with parchment paper.

2. Spread the marinara sauce on one of the tortillas, then top with the mozzarella, dried minced onions, Italian seasoning, and pepperoni. Top with the second tortilla and place on the prepared pan.

3. Bake for 10 to 15 minutes, until the cheese has melted.

4. Slice into four pieces and garnish with green onions, if desired. Enjoy!

ALLERGENS

NOTE: To make this quesadilla gluten-free, use gluten-free tortillas.

SHEET PAN SAUSAGE, PEPPERS & GNOCCHI WITH HOT HONEY SAUCE

YIELD: 2 servings   **PREP TIME:** 5 minutes   **COOK TIME:** 15 minutes

This is one of the easiest dinners I have ever made, and it is so good every time. The garlicky hot honey sauce is really what makes the dish; it adds tangy, sweet, spicy, and salty notes. You can adjust the quantity of honey and Sriracha in the sauce to your liking—some people like it more sweet than spicy, while others like it more spicy than sweet. I'll leave that up to you and your taste buds!

12 ounces smoked sausage links, sliced (see Notes)

1 cup shelf-stable or refrigerated gnocchi

1 cup sliced red bell peppers

½ cup diced yellow onions

SAUCE

3 tablespoons olive oil

1½ tablespoons honey

1 tablespoon Sriracha sauce

1 teaspoon lemon juice

2 teaspoons minced garlic

Pinch of salt

Pinch of ground black pepper

Sliced green onions, for garnish (optional)

1. Preheat the oven to 375°F and line a sheet pan with aluminum foil.

2. Put the sausage, gnocchi, bell peppers, and onions on the prepared sheet pan and mix until evenly distributed.

3. Make the sauce: In a small mixing bowl, whisk together the olive oil, honey, Sriracha, lemon juice, garlic, salt, and pepper until well combined. Drizzle the sauce over the ingredients on the sheet pan and toss until everything is evenly coated.

4. Bake for 15 minutes, or until the sausage is browned and the vegetables are fork-tender. Garnish with green onions, if desired, and enjoy! Best served fresh but can last in the fridge for up to 4 days. To reheat, microwave on high for 1 minute.

NOTES: You can use any smoked sausage you prefer. I used Hillshire Farm Beef Smoked Sausage.

If you'd like to use a toaster oven for this recipe, you can bake the ingredients in two batches on two small sheet pans.

SMOKY CHEESE-STUFFED CHICKEN WITH BROCCOLI

 YIELD: 1 serving   **PREP TIME:** 10 minutes   **COOK TIME:** 25 minutes

Though it's plated with a vegetable to make a balanced, complete meal, the stuffed chicken is the star of this show. The creamy filling is bursting with smoky and savory flavors. This is one of my favorite meals to make when I have a little extra energy for cooking—and the recipe is easy to double to save cooking the next night. Fun fact: The filling makes a good dip as well!

1 boneless, skinless chicken breast (about 6 ounces)

1 teaspoon smoked paprika, divided

Salt and pepper

2 ounces ⅓-less-fat cream cheese (aka Neufchâtel) (¼ cup), softened

¼ cup shredded smoked cheddar cheese

½ teaspoon garlic powder

1 teaspoon dried chives

1 cup frozen broccoli florets or other veggie(s) of choice

2 tablespoons olive oil

Sliced green onions, for garnish (optional)

1. Preheat the toaster oven or oven to 375°F. Line a small sheet pan with parchment paper.

2. Butterfly the chicken breast by cutting it in half horizontally, holding your knife parallel to the cutting board; be careful not to cut all the way through. Season the chicken all over with ½ teaspoon of the smoked paprika and a pinch each of salt and pepper; set aside.

3. In a medium-sized bowl, mix the cream cheese, cheddar cheese, garlic powder, and chives until well combined.

4. Spread the cream cheese mixture on one of the cut sides of the butterflied breast, then fold the other side over the filling, covering it completely.

5. Place the stuffed chicken breast on the prepared sheet pan and arrange the broccoli around the chicken. Drizzle the broccoli with the olive oil and season with the remaining ½ teaspoon of smoked paprika and a pinch each of salt and pepper.

6. Bake for 20 to 25 minutes, or until the chicken reaches an internal temperature of 165°F and the broccoli is fork-tender. Transfer the chicken and broccoli to a serving plate and garnish with green onions, if desired.

ALLERGENS

CABBAGE ROLLS WITH SPICY SOY DIPPING SAUCE

YIELD: 1 serving   **PREP TIME:** 15 minutes, plus overnight to freeze cabbage leaves (not including time to cook rice)   **COOK TIME:** 20 minutes

These Asian-inspired cabbage rolls are a tasty way to get your protein, carb, and veggie intake. This meatless recipe is perfect if you follow a vegan or vegetarian diet as well. For me it's the sauce, with its spicy, savory, and tangy notes, that really makes this dish. I love adding it to the filling as well as using it as a dipping sauce.

6 extra-large green cabbage leaves

SAUCE

3 tablespoons soy sauce

3 tablespoons toasted sesame oil

1 tablespoon unseasoned rice vinegar

1 teaspoon Sriracha sauce

1 teaspoon sesame seeds

1 teaspoon dried minced onions

½ teaspoon garlic powder

¼ teaspoon ginger powder

FILLING

½ cup crumbled firm tofu

½ cup finely diced button mushrooms

½ cup peeled and shredded carrots

¼ cup finely diced yellow onions

½ cup cooked white or brown rice

Olive oil, for the pan

Dried parsley, for garnish

1. Place the cabbage leaves in the freezer overnight. The next day, run hot water over the cabbage to defrost it. This step will make the leaves softer and more pliable.

2. In a small mixing bowl, mix together the ingredients for the sauce until well combined.

3. Make the filling: Put the tofu, mushrooms, carrots, onions, and rice in a medium-sized frying pan and drizzle half of the sauce over the ingredients. Mix until evenly distributed, then cover and cook over medium heat until the vegetables are soft, about 8 minutes.

4. Assemble the rolls: Place an equal amount of the filling mixture along the bottom of each cabbage leaf, about ⅓ heaping cup per leaf. Tuck in the sides and roll to the opposite end, burrito style.

5. Wipe out the pan you used for the filling and grease it lightly with olive oil. Place the cabbage rolls seam side down in the pan and cook over medium-high heat until golden brown, about 6 minutes. Flip the rolls over and cook for another 6 minutes, or until golden brown on the other side. Browning the rolls will seal them so they do not open while eating.

6. Garnish the rolls with dried parsley and enjoy with the other half of the sauce.

NOTE: To make these cabbage rolls gluten-free, use gluten-free soy sauce or tamari.

AIR FRYER SHRIMP KABOBS

 YIELD: 2 servings   **PREP TIME:** 10 minutes   **COOK TIME:** 8 minutes

You can make kabobs with basically any meat and/or vegetable, but shrimp would have to be my favorite. Shrimp is so quick and easy to cook, plus most frozen shrimp is already shelled and deveined, saving you the prep work. Air-frying is such a quick and easy way to cook kabobs too!

1 small red bell pepper

¼ medium red onion

1 small zucchini

12 medium shrimp with tails on, peeled and deveined

2 tablespoons olive oil

1 teaspoon ground dried rosemary

1 teaspoon ground dried oregano

Pinch of salt

Pinch of ground black pepper

Chopped fresh parsley, for garnish (optional)

1 or 2 lemon wedges, for serving (optional)

SPECIAL EQUIPMENT
4 (12-inch) or 6 (8-inch) skewers, depending on size of air fryer

1. If using wooden skewers, soak them in water for 20 minutes. Line the air-fryer basket with parchment paper.

2. Chop the bell pepper and onion into 1-inch squares. Cut the zucchini into ½-inch-thick half-moons.

3. Alternately thread the shrimp and pepper, onion, and zucchini pieces onto the skewers.

4. Drizzle the olive oil over the skewers, then season them with the rosemary, oregano, salt, and pepper.

5. Place the kabobs in the prepared basket and air-fry at 375°F for 8 minutes, or until the shrimp are fully cooked and the vegetables are slightly charred.

6. Garnish with parsley and enjoy with lemon wedges, if desired. Can last in the fridge for up to 4 days. To reheat, microwave on high for 40 seconds. This is also great cold and can be used in a salad.

CHEESY GARLICKY SPAGHETTI SQUASH

OPTION   OPTION

YIELD: 2 servings   **PREP TIME:** 10 minutes   **COOK TIME:** 50 minutes

There is nothing better than jamming your fork into the center of a dish and pulling up a bunch of mouthwatering cheese strings. That's what you get with this recipe. The garlic, cheese, and spaghetti squash work together perfectly, creating an elevated yet simple vegetarian dinner.

1 small spaghetti squash (1½ to 2 pounds)

2 tablespoons olive oil

1 cup fresh spinach

1 cup shredded part-skim mozzarella cheese

½ cup grated Parmesan cheese

2 teaspoons minced garlic

½ cup plain breadcrumbs

2 teaspoons dried parsley

½ teaspoon crushed red pepper

⅛ teaspoon salt

⅛ teaspoon ground black pepper

Chopped fresh parsley, for garnish (optional)

1. Preheat the toaster oven or oven to 400°F. Line a small sheet pan with parchment paper.

2. Cut the spaghetti squash in half lengthwise, scoop out the seeds, and drizzle the cut sides with the olive oil. Place face down on the prepared pan and roast for 35 to 40 minutes, until the flesh is fork-tender. Turn the squash halves over and loosen the strands with a fork.

3. Evenly fill the centers of the squash halves with the spinach, mozzarella, Parmesan, and garlic. Top the squash halves with the breadcrumbs, parsley, crushed red pepper, salt, and black pepper.

4. Bake the stuffed squash for 10 to 15 minutes, until the topping is golden brown. Serve garnished with parsley, if desired. Can last in the fridge for up to 5 days. To reheat, place on a small sheet pan lined with parchment paper and bake in a preheated 400°F oven for 8 to 10 minutes.

ALLERGENS

NOTE: To make this dish vegetarian, use a Parmesan cheese that is not made with animal rennet. To make it gluten-free, use gluten-free breadcrumbs.

ROASTED RED PEPPER SALMON & GREEN BEANS

 YIELD: 1 serving **PREP TIME:** 8 minutes (not including time to cook rice) **COOK TIME:** 25 minutes

This easy recipe is always a hit at dinner parties; it's great for those times when you're cooking for more than just yourself. Simply double, triple, or quadruple the ingredients as needed. Aside from the lemony sauce, the most important ingredient is the roasted red pepper. It elevates the dish perfectly, adding tang and zest. Pair the salmon with green beans and rice and you have a perfectly balanced meal.

LEMON SAUCE

1 tablespoon lemon juice

1 tablespoon olive oil

1 teaspoon minced garlic

Pinch of salt

Pinch of ground black pepper

1 (6-ounce) salmon fillet

4 ounces green beans, trimmed

2 tablespoons olive oil

Pinch of salt

Pinch of ground black pepper

1 jarred roasted red pepper

½ cup cooked white or brown rice, for serving

Dried parsley, for garnish

1. Preheat the toaster oven or oven to 375°F. Line a small sheet pan with parchment paper.

2. Make the sauce: In a small mixing bowl, whisk together the lemon juice, olive oil, garlic, salt, and pepper.

3. Set the salmon and green beans on the prepared pan. Drizzle with the olive oil and season with the salt and pepper, then drizzle with half of the sauce. Top the salmon with the roasted red bell pepper and bake for 20 to 25 minutes, until the fish is flaky and the green beans are tender.

4. Plate the salmon on a bed of rice, with the green beans alongside. Drizzle with the remaining sauce and sprinkle with dried parsley.

CHILI HONEY-GLAZED SALMON & BROCCOLI

OPTION

YIELD: 1 serving   **PREP TIME:** 5 minutes (not including time to cook rice)
COOK TIME: 10 to 20 minutes, depending on method

Who doesn't love a good balance of savory, sweet, and spicy? I know I do! Same with my family. That is why this salmon is one of their top dinner requests. Made with a touch of soy sauce, the sweet, spicy, and savory components of the chili honey glaze are in perfect harmony and complement the salmon nicely. To make a balanced meal, pair the salmon with broccoli and serve it over rice. But you can prepare it with any vegetable you like. You also have the choice of preparing it in an air fryer or in the oven (this is a great one for a toaster oven).

CHILI HONEY GLAZE

2 tablespoons honey

1 tablespoon soy sauce

1 tablespoon olive oil

1 teaspoon minced garlic

1 teaspoon crushed red pepper

1 (6-ounce) salmon fillet

1 cup frozen broccoli florets, defrosted

½ cup cooked white or brown rice, for serving

Sliced green onions, for garnish (optional)

1. Make the glaze: In a small bowl, mix the honey, soy sauce, olive oil, garlic, and crushed red pepper until well combined.

2. *If using an air fryer,* line the air-fryer basket with aluminum foil. *If using the toaster oven or oven,* preheat it to 375°F and line a small sheet pan with foil.

3. Place the salmon in the center of the prepared basket or sheet pan. Arrange the broccoli around the salmon. Drizzle the glaze over the salmon and broccoli.

4. Air-fry at 375°F for 10 minutes or bake in the oven for 15 to 20 minutes, until the salmon is fully cooked; when done, it will flake easily and will have reached an internal temperature of 140°F.

5. Serve with the rice, garnished with green onions, if desired.

NOTE: To make this dish gluten-free, use gluten-free soy sauce or tamari.

COD & BRIE WITH SPICY SAUCE

OPTION

YIELD: 1 serving   **PREP TIME:** 5 minutes (not including time to cook rice)
COOK TIME: 15 to 23 minutes, depending on method

A while ago, I ate at a stunning farm-to-table restaurant where the server recommended a dish similar to this one. At first, I was skeptical because fish and cheese do not tend to pair well, but I thought I would try it anyway. Let me tell you, I am so glad I did. This is my version of that dish, re-created to have a little more flavor balance and require minimal effort. For a balanced meal, serve with a vegetable of your choice. You have the choice of making this in the air fryer or oven.

1 (6-ounce) skinless cod fillet (see Notes)

Pinch of salt

Pinch of ground black pepper

2 slices Brie cheese

½ cup cooked white or brown rice or couscous, for serving

Sliced green onions, for garnish (optional)

SPICY SAUCE

1 tablespoon mayonnaise

1 tablespoon olive oil

1 teaspoon lemon juice

½ teaspoon cayenne pepper

½ teaspoon garlic powder

½ teaspoon paprika

1. *If using an air fryer,* line the air-fryer basket with aluminum foil. *If using the toaster oven or oven,* preheat it to 375°F and line a small sheet pan with foil.

2. Set the cod fillet in the prepared basket or pan. Season the cod with the salt and pepper and air-fry at 350°F for 10 minutes or bake in the oven for 10 to 15 minutes.

3. Top the fish with the Brie and air-fry for another 5 minutes or bake for another 5 to 8 minutes, until the cheese has melted and the cod is fully cooked. When done, the fish will flake easily and will have reached an internal temperature of 140°F.

4. While the cod is cooking, make the sauce: Put the mayonnaise, olive oil, lemon juice, cayenne, garlic powder, and paprika in a small bowl and mix until well combined.

5. Plate the cod on a bed of rice or couscous and drizzle with the sauce. Garnish with green onions, if desired, and enjoy!

NOTES: Salmon or haddock fillets would also work well in this recipe.

To make this dish gluten-free, serve it over rice rather than couscous. To make it egg-free, use vegan mayo.

ALLERGENS

OPTION

PARMESAN-CRUSTED TILAPIA & ASPARAGUS

YIELD: 1 serving **PREP TIME:** 5 minutes (not including time to cook couscous)
COOK TIME: 10 to 20 minutes, depending on method

Cheap, easy, and quick—this recipe is perfect for those days when you are hungry and want a healthy meal but are too energy depleted to make something elaborate. I pair the fish with pearl couscous and asparagus to make a complete and balanced dinner; you could always swap in another vegetable according to what's in season. Pearl couscous takes longer to cook than ordinary couscous, so if you're looking for a super fast meal, save the pearl couscous for another night.

1 (5-ounce) tilapia fillet

Salt and pepper

¼ cup plain breadcrumbs

¼ cup grated Parmesan cheese

1 tablespoon dried parsley, divided

½ teaspoon garlic powder, divided

4 medium-thick asparagus spears, tough ends removed

½ cup cooked pearl or ordinary couscous, for serving

Lemon slice, for serving (optional)

1. *If using the toaster oven or oven,* preheat it to 375°F and line a small sheet pan with parchment paper. *If using an air fryer,* line the air-fryer basket with parchment paper.

2. Pat the tilapia dry with a paper towel. Season the fish with a pinch each of salt and pepper; set aside.

3. Make the Parmesan coating: In a medium-sized bowl, mix the breadcrumbs, Parmesan cheese, 1½ teaspoons of the parsley, and ¼ teaspoon of the garlic powder until well combined.

4. Coat the tilapia in the breadcrumb mixture, then place it in the prepared basket or sheet pan. Spray the fish with cooking oil spray.

5. Place the asparagus next to the tilapia, then spray it with cooking oil spray and season with a pinch each of salt and pepper and the remaining 1½ teaspoons of parsley and ¼ teaspoon of garlic powder.

6. Air-fry at 350°F for 10 minutes or bake in the oven for 15 to 20 minutes. When done, the asparagus will be fork-tender; the tilapia will flake easily and will have reached an internal temperature of 140°F.

7. Serve over couscous, topped with a lemon slice, if desired.

ALLERGENS

SHEET PAN CHICKEN & BROCCOLI WITH SPICY GINGER SOY SAUCE

OPTION

YIELD: 1 serving   **PREP TIME:** 10 minutes (not including time to cook rice)
COOK TIME: 20 minutes

Looking for a simple sheet pan dinner? Well, here is one for you! The zesty, lightly spicy sauce is one of my favorites to use with meat, especially chicken. You can put it on any meat or veggie and it will elevate the whole dish. If you have time, I recommend marinating the chicken in the sauce for half an hour before cooking for maximum flavor. Green beans are another veggie that pairs well with this chicken dish.

1 boneless, skinless chicken breast (about 6 ounces)

1 cup frozen broccoli florets, defrosted

½ cup cooked white or brown rice, for serving

Sliced green onions, for garnish (optional)

SAUCE

2 tablespoons soy sauce

2 tablespoons toasted sesame oil

1 teaspoon sesame seeds

1 teaspoon minced garlic

½ teaspoon ginger powder

¼ teaspoon crushed red pepper

1. Preheat the toaster oven or oven to 400°F. Line a small sheet pan with aluminum foil or parchment paper.

2. Pound the chicken breast until it is even in thickness and slightly thinner overall.

3. Make the sauce: In a small bowl, mix the soy sauce, sesame oil, sesame seeds, garlic, ginger powder, and crushed red pepper until well combined.

4. Place the chicken and broccoli on the prepared pan and drizzle the sauce evenly over them.

5. Bake for 15 to 20 minutes, until the internal temperature of the chicken has reached 165°F and the broccoli is tender.

6. Enjoy over rice, garnished with green onions, if desired.

NOTE: To make this dish gluten-free, use gluten-free soy sauce or tamari.

ONE-POT CREAMY TOMATO PASTA

OPTION

YIELD: 2 servings **PREP TIME:** 5 minutes **COOK TIME:** 25 minutes

Calling all pasta lovers! Instead of using one pot to cook the pasta and another to make the sauce, here you need only one pot. Not only does this dish taste amazing, but it saves you time on cleaning dishes, and who doesn't love that?

⅔ cup chicken broth

½ cup half-and-half

½ cup tomato sauce

1 tablespoon tomato paste

1 tablespoon olive oil

1 cup rotini, rigatoni, or penne pasta

¼ cup grated Parmesan cheese, plus more for garnish

¼ cup shredded part-skim mozzarella cheese

½ teaspoon ground dried thyme

Salt and pepper

1. In a medium-sized saucepan, bring the broth, half-and-half, tomato sauce, tomato paste, and olive oil to a low boil over medium-high heat, stirring until the paste has dissolved.

2. Once the mixture starts to boil, add the pasta, cover, and cook for 12 minutes, or until the pasta is al dente.

3. Reduce the heat to medium-low and stir in the Parmesan, mozzarella, and thyme. Cook until the sauce has thickened and the cheese has melted, 5 to 10 minutes. Season to taste with salt and pepper, keeping in mind that the Parmesan topping will contribute some additional salt.

4. Serve garnished with Parmesan. Best served fresh but can last in the fridge for up to 5 days. To reheat, microwave on high for 1½ minutes.

ALLERGENS

NOTE: To make this dish gluten-free, use a gluten-free pasta.

HIDDEN VEGGIE PASTA

  YIELD: 2 servings   **PREP TIME:** 15 minutes   **COOK TIME:** 25 minutes

This recipe is for those of you who are reluctant vegetable eaters or have picky children who do not like vegetables. I find that blending vegetables into a sauce and mixing in some seasonings helps mask their texture and flavor. The next smart move is to serve the sauce over pasta (since everyone loves pasta!). Feel free to adjust the seasonings to suit your taste (or the picky member of your family).

Salt

1 cup rotini, rigatoni, or penne pasta

1 medium tomato, coarsely chopped

1 small yellow summer squash, coarsely chopped

1 small red bell pepper, coarsely chopped

¼ medium yellow onion, coarsely chopped

1 tablespoon chopped fresh parsley

½ teaspoon dried ground oregano

½ teaspoon dried ground thyme

½ teaspoon garlic powder

Pinch of ground black pepper

FOR GARNISH (OPTIONAL)

Fresh basil leaves

Grated Parmesan cheese

ALLERGENS

OPTION

1. Bring a pot of salted water to a boil and cook the pasta until al dente, following the package directions. Reserve ¼ cup of the pasta cooking water, then drain the pasta and set aside.

2. Put the tomato, squash, bell pepper, and onion in a blender and puree until you have a smooth, thick sauce.

3. Pour the sauce into the pot you used to cook the pasta. Season with a pinch of salt along with the parsley, oregano, thyme, garlic powder, and pepper. Cook over medium heat for 10 minutes, or until steam starts to roll off the surface of the sauce.

4. Return the pasta and pasta water to the pot with the sauce and mix gently until all the rotini is coated in the sauce.

5. If desired, garnish with fresh basil and Parmesan cheese. Best served fresh but can last in the fridge for up to 4 days. To reheat, microwave on high for 30 seconds.

NOTE: To make this dish vegan and dairy-free, omit the Parmesan cheese or use a vegan replacement, such as nutritional yeast. (Traditional Parmesan is made with animal rennet, so it is not vegetarian, either.) To make it gluten-free, use a gluten-free pasta.

HEALING CHICKEN NOODLE SOUP

OPTION

YIELD: 2 servings   **PREP TIME:** 12 minutes   **COOK TIME:** 2 hours 45 minutes or 5 hours 45 minutes

Feeling stuffy and under the weather? This spicy version of the classic chicken noodle soup will open your nasal passages and have you feeling better instantly. It's the addition of crushed red pepper and chili oil that does it! The turmeric is there for its healing powers too. Easy to make, this is the perfect lazy-day soup. If you are super sick, you can use precut frozen vegetables so you don't have to chop anything. I've used bowtie pasta instead of the traditional egg noodles, but feel free to use any pasta or noodles you like.

2 boneless, skinless chicken breasts (about 12 ounces)

3 cups chicken broth

½ cup peeled and diced carrots

½ cup diced celery

½ cup diced yellow onions

½ cup fresh spinach

1 teaspoon dried parsley

½ teaspoon garlic powder

½ teaspoon crushed red pepper

½ teaspoon turmeric powder

1 tablespoon chili oil

1 tablespoon unsalted butter

¾ cup bowtie pasta

Sliced green onions, for garnish (optional)

1. Put the chicken in a slow cooker and pour in the broth. Cook for 1½ hours on high or 3 hours on low, or until the chicken is cooked through (the temperature in the thickest part of the breast should read 165°F).

2. Take out the chicken and pull it apart with two forks.

3. Return the chicken to the slow cooker and add the rest of the ingredients, except for the pasta. Continue to cook for 1 hour on high or 2¼ hours on low.

4. Add the pasta and cook until it is al dente, about 15 minutes on high or 30 minutes on low.

5. Ladle the soup into bowls and garnish with sliced green onions, if desired. Best served fresh but can last in the fridge for up to 4 days. To reheat, microwave on high for 1 minute 30 seconds.

ALLERGENS

NOTE: To make this dish gluten-free, use a gluten-free pasta.

SOUL-WARMING HAM & POTATO SOUP

 YIELD: 2 servings   **PREP TIME:** 10 minutes   **COOK TIME:** 3 or 6 hours

All soups are soul-warming in a way, but this soup is about as soul-warming as they come. Where I'm from, ham, cheese, and potatoes are some of the top comfort foods to eat during the winter, especially after a day of skiing at the Elk Mountain Ski Resort, which is right next to my hometown of Union Dale, Pennsylvania. Those three key ingredients make this the ultimate comfort soup.

3 cups chicken broth

½ cup half-and-half or unsweetened canned coconut cream or milk of choice

1 medium all-purpose potato (such as Yukon Gold or Red Gold), chopped

¼ cup chopped yellow onions

¼ cup chopped ham

3 tablespoons bacon bits, plus more for garnish if desired

1 teaspoon dried minced onions

½ teaspoon garlic powder

Pinch of ground black pepper

¼ cup shredded cheddar cheese, for garnish

1 tablespoon sliced green onions, for garnish (optional)

1. Put the broth, half-and-half, potato, and onions in a slow cooker. Cook for 2 hours on high or 4 hours on low.

2. Add the ham, bacon bits, dried minced onions, garlic powder, and pepper and continue to cook for 1 hour on high or 2 hours on low.

3. Ladle the soup into bowls and sprinkle with the cheese. If desired, garnish with bacon bits and/or sliced green onions. Best served fresh but can last in the fridge for up to 4 days. To reheat, microwave on high for 1 minute.

ALLERGENS

CREAMY TORTELLINI SOUP

YIELD: 3 servings   PREP TIME: 10 minutes   COOK TIME: 2 hours 45 minutes or 5½ hours

One of my favorite things to do after a long day is saddle up to a warm bowl of hearty, nourishing soup. This creamy and flavorful tomato-based tortellini soup delivers on that score as well as being incredibly comforting. It will leave you feeling full and cozy inside.

2 cups tomato sauce

2 cups chicken broth

½ cup half-and-half

2 tablespoons olive oil

Pinch of ground black pepper

1 cup fresh spinach

½ cup diced yellow onions

½ cup diced red bell peppers

2 cups cheese tortellini

3 tablespoons grated Parmesan cheese, plus more for garnish

Chopped fresh parsley, for garnish (optional)

1. In a slow cooker, stir together the tomato sauce, broth, half-and-half, olive oil, and black pepper. Add the spinach, onions, and bell peppers and stir to combine. Cook for 2½ hours on high or 5 hours on low.

2. Add the tortellini and Parmesan cheese and cook until the tortellini is soft, another 15 minutes on high or 30 minutes on low. When the tortellini is sufficiently cooked, you'll be able to easily cut through it with a fork.

3. Serve immediately, garnished with Parmesan cheese and, if desired, fresh parsley. Best served fresh but can last in the fridge for up to 4 days. To reheat, microwave on high for 1 minute 30 seconds.

ALLERGENS

HEARTY TURKEY CHILI

 YIELD: 6 servings   **PREP TIME:** 15 minutes   **COOK TIME:** 2 or 4 hours

Chili is usually made with beef, but I find there is something about ground turkey that makes it taste better. Not only does turkey offer a more tender texture, but it is also a leaner protein, having a lower saturated fat content. Chickpeas aren't a traditional choice for chili, but I love the heartiness they give to this recipe. Using a slow cooker is a lifesaver as well because you do not have to keep checking on it. Just throw all the ingredients into the cooker, come back in four or five hours, and it is done! You could also make this ahead and keep it warm in the slow cooker to serve at a tailgate.

24 ounces ground turkey

1 medium green bell pepper, chopped

1 medium red bell pepper, chopped

1 small yellow onion, chopped

1 jalapeño pepper, finely chopped

1 tablespoon minced garlic

3 cups marinara sauce

3 cups chicken broth

1 (15-ounce) can chickpeas, rinsed and drained

1 (15-ounce) can black beans

2 tablespoons chili powder

1 teaspoon ground cumin

1 teaspoon ground black pepper

½ teaspoon onion powder

3 tablespoons olive oil

FOR SERVING (OPTIONAL)

½ cup shredded cheddar cheese

¼ cup chopped green onions

1. Put the turkey in a slow cooker and break it up a little bit, then add the bell peppers, onion, jalapeño, and garlic.

2. Pour the marinara sauce and broth into the slow cooker, then add the chickpeas, black beans, chili powder, cumin, pepper, onion powder, and olive oil and stir to combine.

3. Cook for 2 hours on high or 4 hours on low, or until the meat is thoroughly cooked and the chili has thickened. Serve topped with cheddar cheese and/or sliced green onions, if desired.

4. Best served fresh but can last in the fridge for up to 4 days. To reheat, microwave on high for 1 minute 30 seconds.

ALLERGENS

OPTION

NOTE: To make this chili dairy-free, omit the cheese topping.

COMFORTING WINTER SOUP

 YIELD: 3 servings   **PREP TIME:** 10 minutes   **COOK TIME:** 4 or 8 hours

During fall and winter, seasonal squash seems to be the most popular produce. It's understandable because winter squash is super tasty, budget-friendly, and can last for months. One of my favorite recipes to make with squash is this comforting soup. Winter squash pairs beautifully with sausage, and that combination is the inspiration for this recipe.

16 ounces smoked sausage, sliced (about 2 cups) (see Note)

2 cups peeled and chopped butternut squash

1 cup fresh spinach

1 small yellow onion, diced

6 cups beef broth

1 tablespoon smoked paprika

1½ teaspoons ground black pepper

1 teaspoon garlic powder

Put all of the ingredients in a slow cooker. Cook for 4 hours on high or 8 hours on low, or until the squash is fully tender. Best served fresh but can last in the fridge for up to 4 days. To reheat, microwave on high for 1 minute.

NOTE: You can use any smoked sausage you prefer. I used Hillshire Farm Beef Smoked Sausage.

BBQ PULLED CHICKEN SANDWICHES

OPTION

YIELD: 4 servings   **PREP TIME:** 5 minutes   **COOK TIME:** 1½ or 3½ hours

Who doesn't love a good barbecue chicken sandwich—especially when it is this easy to make? That's why this is one of my favorite recipes in this book. It's perfect when you are drained from the day's activities but want a comforting and filling meal. It makes a great potluck or tailgating dish too. After you try it, I'm sure it will be one of your favorites as well!

1¼ cups BBQ sauce

½ cup chicken broth

2 tablespoons olive oil

½ teaspoon garlic powder

Pinch of ground black pepper

3 boneless, skinless chicken breasts (about 18 ounces)

4 hamburger buns, for serving

1. Put the BBQ sauce, broth, olive oil, garlic powder, and pepper in a slow cooker and stir to combine. Add the chicken and turn to coat in the sauce. Cook for 1½ hours on high or 3 hours on low, or until the chicken is cooked all the way through (the temperature should reach 165°F in the thickest part of the chicken).

2. Take out the chicken and pull it apart with two forks. Return the chicken to the slow cooker and mix with the sauce.

3. Enjoy the pulled chicken on buns. Once assembled, the sandwiches are best served fresh, but the pulled chicken can last in the fridge for up to 4 days. To reheat, microwave on high for 1 minute.

ALLERGENS

NOTE: To make these sandwiches gluten-free, use gluten-free buns.

CHICKEN TIKKA MASALA

 YIELD: 1 serving   **PREP TIME:** 10 minutes (not including time to cook rice)
COOK TIME: 2 or 3 hours

This recipe is perfect for those cold and snowy days when you want to cozy up to a soul-warming meal. Even better, it takes minimal effort to make. All you do is throw the ingredients into a slow cooker, and you have a meal in as little as 2 hours.

½ cup diced yellow onions

½ cup unsweetened canned coconut cream or half-and-half

¼ cup plain Greek yogurt

¾ teaspoon garam masala

¼ teaspoon ginger powder

¼ teaspoon paprika

¼ teaspoon turmeric powder

¼ teaspoon ground black pepper

¼ teaspoon salt

1 boneless, skinless chicken breast (about 6 ounces), cubed

1 cup fresh spinach

½ cup cooked white or brown rice, for serving

Chopped fresh cilantro, for garnish (optional)

1. In a slow cooker, stir together the onions, coconut cream, yogurt, spices, and salt until well combined. Add the chicken and toss to coat with the yogurt mixture. Cook for 1½ hours on high or 2½ hours on low, or until the chicken is cooked through.

2. At the 1½-hour (or 2½-hour) mark, stir in the spinach, then cook for another 30 minutes on high or 1 hour on low, or until the spinach is wilted.

3. Serve over rice and garnish with fresh cilantro, if desired.

ALLERGENS

TAVERN POT ROAST

YIELD: 2 servings   **PREP TIME:** 10 minutes   **COOK TIME:** 2½ or 5½ hours

Whenever I make this recipe, I feel like I have been transported back in time to an old English tavern. This is my take on the classic pot roast with an easier twist, all thanks to the handy-dandy slow cooker. Don't discard the delicious and nutritious cooking broth! It's meant to be served with the meat and vegetables, like the French pot-au-feu or the less glamorous sounding New England boiled dinner. In this rustic recipe, I simply scrub the potatoes and carrots; however, if you're not using organic produce, I suggest you peel them.

1 (12-ounce) piece boneless beef chuck roast (see Note)

1 cup chopped yellow onions

1 cup coarsely chopped red potatoes

½ cup coarsely chopped carrots

2 cups beef broth

½ cup red wine

1½ teaspoons Worcestershire sauce

2 tablespoons tomato paste

1 tablespoon olive oil

2 bay leaves

1 teaspoon ground dried thyme

½ teaspoon garlic powder

Pinch of ground black pepper

1. Put the beef, onions, potatoes, and carrots in a slow cooker. Add the rest of the ingredients and stir to combine.

2. Cook for 2½ hours on high or 5½ hours on low, or until the meat is fork-tender and pulls apart easily.

3. Serve in shallow bowls with the broth. Best served fresh but can last in the fridge for up to 4 days. To reheat, microwave on high for 1 minute 30 seconds.

NOTES: Boneless chuck roast is normally sold in 2-pound pieces or larger. You can ask your butcher to cut off a 12-ounce portion for you, or break down a larger piece yourself and freeze the leftover portion for later. (Looking for another way to use this cut of meat? Check out my Birria Tacos on page 202.)

To make this dish gluten-free, use a gluten-free Worcestershire sauce.

GARLIC CHICKEN PARM PASTA

OPTION

YIELD: 4 servings   **PREP TIME:** 5 minutes   **COOK TIME:** 2 or 4½ hours

If you love pasta like I do, then this recipe is for you. This creamy, savory dish will have your mouth watering and leave you feeling full and satisfied. Beware, though—it is addictive!

2 boneless, skinless chicken breasts (about 12 ounces)

½ cup milk of choice

½ cup chicken broth

⅔ cup grated Parmesan cheese

⅔ cup shredded white cheddar cheese

1 teaspoon minced garlic

¾ teaspoon ground dried oregano

Pinch of salt

Pinch of ground black pepper

2 cups rigatoni or other short pasta of choice

Chopped fresh parsley, for garnish (optional)

1. Put the chicken in a slow cooker, then pour in the milk and broth. Sprinkle on the Parmesan, cheddar, garlic, oregano, salt, and pepper. Cook for 2 hours on high or 4½ hours on low, or until the chicken is cooked all the way through.

2. About 15 minutes before the chicken is done, bring a pot of salted water to a boil and cook the pasta until al dente, following the package directions. Drain well.

3. Once the chicken is done, take it out and pull it apart with two forks. Return the chicken to the slow cooker and add the cooked pasta. Mix until well coated in the sauce.

4. Serve garnished with fresh parsley, if desired. Best served fresh but can last in the fridge for up to 4 days. To reheat, microwave on high for 1 minute 30 seconds.

ALLERGENS

NOTE: To make this dish gluten-free, use a gluten-free pasta.

CLASSIC SLOPPY JOES

OPTION

YIELD: 3 servings **PREP TIME:** 5 minutes **COOK TIME:** 2 or 4½ hours

Sloppy joes are a staple in my household because of how convenient and filling they are. It's hard to imagine a more comforting and nostalgic meal. This is a great recipe to meal prep on a Sunday evening so that it's ready for you to heat up after a long day of work or school on Monday. And it requires just one pot—a slow cooker—so the cleanup is easy. One of my pickiest family members, an eight-year-old, absolutely loved these delicious sandwiches, so it's safe to say that they are kid-friendly too, making this an ideal family dinner. I like brioche buns for this recipe (and so did the eight-year-old), but any type of hamburger bun will work. I serve the sloppy joes with fried pork rinds or chips.

1 pound (93% lean) ground beef

½ cup diced yellow onions

⅔ cup ketchup

2 tablespoons Dijon mustard

1 tablespoon Worcestershire sauce

1 tablespoon brown sugar

½ teaspoon garlic powder

½ teaspoon onion powder

¼ teaspoon salt

½ teaspoon ground black pepper

3 brioche buns or other hamburger buns, for serving

1. Put the ground beef and onions in a slow cooker and break up the meat with a fork. Cook for 1 hour on high or 2¼ hours on low, or until the beef is mostly cooked and the onions are translucent.

2. Add the rest of the ingredients and mix until well combined. Cook for another hour on high or another 2¼ hours on low, stirring halfway through cooking. When done, the beef will be fully cooked and the mixture will be slightly thickened.

3. Serve the meat filling on buns. Best served fresh, but the filling can last in the fridge, stored separately from the buns, for up to 4 days. To reheat, assemble a sandwich and microwave on high for about 40 seconds.

ALLERGENS

OPTION

NOTE: To make these sandwiches gluten-free, use a gluten-free Worcestershire sauce and gluten-free buns. To make them egg-free, use egg-free buns. (Brioche buns often contain egg.)

EASY-PEASY DINNERS SLOW AND STEADY

BIRRIA TACOS

 YIELD: 2 servings   **PREP TIME:** 12 minutes   **COOK TIME:** 3 or 6 hours

Nothing beats a delicious Mexican birria taco, but why do they have to be so labor-intensive? Traditionally, you need to make an adobo sauce before you can even begin stewing the meat. Then, before serving, you pan-fry each taco—just for them to be devoured in 15 minutes and leaving you with a million pots and pans to clean. Here, using a slow cooker and an air fryer, I show you how to make the best birria tacos with less effort and less cleanup.

BIRRIA FILLING

½ small yellow onion, peeled

1½ cups beef broth

½ cup water

½ cup tomato sauce

2 teaspoons minced garlic

1 teaspoon crushed red pepper

½ teaspoon ground cumin

½ teaspoon turmeric powder

½ teaspoon ground dried thyme

2 bay leaves

1 (12-ounce) piece boneless beef chuck roast (see Note, page 196)

4 (5-inch) yellow corn tortillas

½ cup shredded Monterey Jack cheese, divided

Chopped fresh cilantro, for garnish (optional)

1. Using the large holes on the side of a box grater, grate the onion. Put the grated onion along with the rest of the filling ingredients, except the beef, in a slow cooker. Stir until everything is well combined, then add the meat and turn it until it is well coated.

2. Cook for 2½ hours on high or 5½ hours on low, or until the meat is thoroughly cooked; it will be tender and pull apart easily.

3. Once the meat is fork-tender, use two forks to pull it apart. Line the air-fryer basket with parchment paper.

4. Dip a tortilla into the slow cooker, coating it in the sauce. Place on a plate, cover with a damp paper towel, and microwave on high for 30 seconds to soften it. Place the coated tortilla in the prepared air-fryer basket. Sprinkle 2 tablespoons of cheese across the entire tortilla, then top one half of the tortilla with one-quarter of the shredded beef. Fold the other half of the tortilla over the meat to form a taco and air-fry at 385°F for 8 minutes, flipping halfway through. When done, the taco will be slightly crispy and hold its shape. (*Note:* Depending on the size of your air fryer, you may be able to cook two tacos at a time.)

5. Repeat with the remaining tortillas, cheese, and beef.

6. Garnish the tacos with fresh cilantro, if desired, and serve with a small cup of the birria sauce for dipping.

7. Store leftover tortillas, filling, and sauce separately in the fridge for up to 4 days. Before assembling and air-frying the tacos, warm the sauce in a shallow bowl in the microwave on high for 1½ minutes and microwave the meat filling on high for 1 minute.

ALLERGENS

NOTE: To crisp the tacos on the stovetop instead of in an air fryer, place a sauced tortilla in a greased frying pan over medium-high heat and assemble the taco as described in Step 4. Cook, flipping halfway through; a couple of minutes per side should do it.

chapter 5:

SWEET TREATS

It's time to unwind, settle in under your favorite blanket, put on your favorite show, and enjoy a comforting dessert. No matter what you're in the mood for, this chapter has you covered. First, you'll find simple recipes with minimal ingredients that come together fast, providing a quick fix for your sweet tooth cravings. Then, in the Indulgent Treats section, you'll find richer, more decadent desserts that may require a few additional ingredients or a little more time to make (but not much more, I promise!). This chapter includes all my favorite desserts from the days when I was restricted to a toaster oven, microwave, and air fryer. I hope you find these recipes as helpful and enjoyable as I do!

COOKIES & CREAM FROZEN YOGURT

OPTION

YIELD: 2 servings   **PREP TIME:** 2 minutes, plus 4 hours to freeze

Cookies and cream is a classic flavor when it comes to ice cream and chocolate bars. This recipe takes the theme to a whole new level, especially since it requires only three ingredients and is so easy to make. Be sure to use full-fat yogurt for extra creaminess.

1 cup full-fat vanilla-flavored Greek yogurt

2 tablespoons honey

3 cream-filled chocolate sandwich cookies, crushed

1. Put the yogurt, honey, and crushed cookies in a medium-sized freezer-safe bowl and mix until well combined.

2. Cover the bowl with plastic wrap and place in the freezer. Freeze for 1 hour, then take out and stir. Freeze for another 3 hours or overnight.

3. Allow the frozen yogurt to soften slightly on the counter before serving. If your sweet tooth can't wait, microwave it using the defrost setting, checking it every 20 seconds, until the yogurt is spoonable. Store leftover frozen yogurt in a tightly sealed container in the freezer for up to 2 weeks.

ALLERGENS

NOTE: To make this dessert gluten-free, use gluten-free chocolate sandwich cookies.

FROZEN BLUEBERRY & NUT CLUSTERS

YIELD: 3 servings   **PREP TIME:** 2 minutes, plus 30 minutes to freeze
COOK TIME: 1 minute

If you are looking for a light dessert or snack that stores well for several days, then this recipe is perfect for you. It works with any kind of chocolate, fruit, and nuts, so feel free to adjust the ingredients to your taste buds. Dark chocolate, blueberries, and cashews are my favorite mixture; I highly recommend you try it!

¾ cup dark chocolate chips

1 tablespoon refined coconut oil

¼ cup frozen blueberries

¼ cup roasted mixed nuts or nuts of choice

1. Put the chocolate chips and coconut oil in a medium-sized microwave-safe bowl and microwave on high, stirring every 20 seconds, until melted, about 1 minute.

2. Add the frozen blueberries and nuts to the melted chocolate mixture and stir gently until the berries and nuts are evenly coated and the chocolate is evenly distributed.

3. Line a sheet pan with parchment paper and spoon the mixture onto the pan in 2-inch clusters. Freeze for 30 minutes. Transfer to a freezer bag and store in the freezer for up to 2 weeks.

ALLERGENS

OPTION

NOTE: To make these clusters dairy-free and vegan, use vegan chocolate chips.

CINNAMON SUGAR PIE CRUSTIES

OPTION

YIELD: 3 servings   **PREP TIME:** 8 minutes   **COOK TIME:** 15 minutes

This idea came about when I was making a pie and had leftover pie crust and egg wash that I didn't want to waste. I decided to cut the crust into strips, brush them with the leftover egg wash, and sprinkle them with cinnamon and sugar. It turned out to be the perfect light dessert.

1 large egg

1 refrigerated pie crust

¼ cup granulated sugar

1½ teaspoons ground cinnamon

1. Preheat the toaster oven or oven to 350°F. Line a small sheet pan with parchment paper or aluminum foil.

2. In a small bowl, whisk the egg until the yolk and white are well combined.

3. Slice the pie crust into 3 by 1½-inch strips. Brush the strips with the whisked egg and sprinkle with the sugar and cinnamon.

4. Lay the strips on the prepared pan. Bake for 12 to 15 minutes, until golden brown.

5. The crusties are best served fresh but can last in the fridge for up to 1 week. Leftover crusties can be eaten cold or warm. To reheat, microwave on high for 30 seconds.

ALLERGENS

OPTION

NOTE: To make these crusties vegetarian, use a pie crust made without animal fat; to make them dairy-free, use a crust made without butter.

BROWN SUGAR TOAST BITES

OPTION

YIELD: 1 serving **PREP TIME:** 5 minutes
COOK TIME: 3 to 7 minutes, depending on method

If Cinnamon Toast Crunch cereal and croutons had a baby, the result might be these toast bites. They're sweet, warm, and crunchy—perfect for indulging your sweet tooth and keeping you satiated until your next meal. I highly recommend eating these with a chocolate hazelnut spread for an extra kick of flavor. You can make them on the stovetop or in an air fryer.

2 slices whole wheat bread

1½ tablespoons unsalted butter, melted

3 tablespoons brown sugar

½ teaspoon ground cinnamon

Powdered sugar, for garnish (optional)

1. Cut the slices of bread into 1-inch squares and put in a medium-sized bowl; set aside.

2. In a small bowl, stir together the melted butter, brown sugar, and cinnamon.

3. Pour the melted butter mixture over the bread and stir until the bread pieces are evenly coated.

4. *To cook the toast bites on a hot plate or the stovetop,* grease a medium-sized frying pan with cooking oil spray and set over medium-low heat. Transfer the coated bread to the pan and cook, tossing periodically, until both sides are golden brown, 3 to 5 minutes.

To cook the toast bites in an air fryer, line the air-fryer basket with parchment paper. Transfer the coated bread pieces to the prepared basket and air-fry at 370°F for 7 minutes, or until golden brown.

5. If desired, dust the toast bites with powdered sugar before serving. They are best enjoyed immediately but can last in the fridge for up to 2 days. To reheat, microwave on high for 30 seconds.

ALLERGENS

NOTES: If you're preparing the toast bites on the stovetop and prefer to use a nonstick pan, you can skip the step of greasing the pan in Step 4.

To make these bites gluten-free, use a gluten-free bread.

CHOCOLATE PROTEIN CHEESECAKE DIP

  YIELD: 1 serving **PREP TIME:** 2 minutes, plus 1 hour to chill

Craving something chocolatey and creamy but don't want something super heavy? Then this dip is for you! It is also the ideal post-workout snack if you're trying to add muscle. The mixture of whipped cream cheese, chocolate protein powder, and honey creates a perfect high-protein sweet snack. I like to serve this dip with pretzels, strawberries, graham crackers, or apple slices, but it's versatile and will likely work with whatever you prefer to pair it with.

⅔ cup whipped cream cheese, room temperature

½ scoop chocolate-flavored protein powder (about 2 teaspoons)

1½ tablespoons honey

½ teaspoon vanilla extract

Put the cream cheese, protein powder, honey, and vanilla in a medium-sized bowl and mix until well combined. Refrigerate for 1 hour before serving. Leftover dip can last in the fridge for up to 5 days.

CREAMY VANILLA DOUBLE PROTEIN DIP

  YIELD: 1 serving   **PREP TIME:** 5 minutes

Who doesn't love a sweet and creamy dip to go with fruit? I know I do, especially when it contains protein to keep me extra full! Made with a blend of cream cheese and Greek yogurt, this protein-rich recipe is super simple to make, and it pairs perfectly with almost any kind of fruit (I find the fruits that work best are strawberries, grapes, or apples) or sweet crackers like graham crackers.

2 ounces ⅓-less-fat cream cheese (aka Neufchâtel) (¼ cup), softened

¼ cup vanilla-flavored Greek yogurt

½ scoop vanilla-flavored protein powder (about 2 teaspoons)

1 teaspoon honey

½ teaspoon ground cinnamon, plus more for garnish

½ teaspoon vanilla extract

1. In a medium-sized mixing bowl, stir together the cream cheese and yogurt until well combined.

2. Mix in the protein powder, honey, cinnamon, and vanilla until well blended.

3. Sprinkle the top with cinnamon and serve. Store leftovers covered in the fridge for up to 5 days; allow the refrigerated dip to soften on the counter for about 15 minutes before eating.

ALLERGENS

OPTION

NOTE: To make this dip egg-free, use a protein powder that is not made from egg whites.

DATE CARAMEL DIP

  YIELD: 2 servings **PREP TIME:** 15 minutes

I love dates. They are a very versatile food with sweet molasses-like notes that pair well with lots of ingredients and flavors, though they go especially well with chocolate, nuts, and fresh fruit. Although this is not an authentic caramel dip, the taste is close. Pair it with apple slices or graham crackers, and you will be just as addicted to this dip as I am.

1 cup pitted Medjool dates

¼ cup hot water

1 tablespoon maple syrup

1 teaspoon vanilla extract

Pinch of ground cinnamon

Pinch of salt

1. Put the dates in a medium-sized bowl and pour the hot water over them. Let the dates sit for 10 minutes.

2. Place the soaked dates, half of the soaking water, the maple syrup, vanilla, cinnamon, and salt in a mini food processor or blender and blend until smooth and creamy.

3. The dip is best served fresh but can last in the fridge for up to 5 days.

BITCHIN' BARK

YIELD: 3 servings **PREP TIME:** 5 minutes, plus 30 minutes to freeze
COOK TIME: 8 minutes

This bark recipe has earned the "bitchin'" description because of how delicious and irresistible it is. It is sure to become your next favorite sweet snack. The best thing about it is that it will last in the freezer for up to two weeks, which means that whenever you need a sweet snack, you can find it ready and waiting for you.

2 (2-ounce) dark chocolate bars

3 tablespoons creamy natural peanut butter

4 caramel chews

¼ cup raspberries (fresh or frozen)

¼ cup mini pretzel twists

Salt

1. Preheat the toaster oven or oven to 300°F and line a small sheet pan with parchment paper.

2. Place the chocolate bars side by side in the pan. Dollop the peanut butter evenly across the tops of the bars. Then scatter the caramel chews and berries evenly over the top.

3. Bake until the chocolate, peanut butter, and caramels are melting, 5 to 8 minutes.

4. Remove the pan from the oven and swirl the peanut butter and caramel with a toothpick, then top with the pretzels and a sprinkle of salt. Allow to cool to room temperature, then freeze for 30 minutes, or until the bark has solidified.

5. Break the frozen bark into pieces with your hands. It is best eaten directly from the freezer.

ALLERGENS

NOTE: To make this bark gluten-free, use gluten-free pretzels. To make it dairy-free, use vegan chocolate.

RASPBERRY-FILLED FROZEN YOGURT BITES

  YIELD: 2 servings   **PREP TIME:** 10 minutes, plus 5 hours to freeze

There is no denying the popularity of frozen yogurt bark—it even went viral on social media. But have you ever thought of making frozen yogurt *bites*? Not only are they easier to portion out, but they're also simpler to make because you just dollop the yogurt mixture into paper cups. These bites are sweet, creamy, and tangy, with earthy notes thanks to the almonds. They are one of my favorite simple sweet snacks.

1 cup vanilla-flavored Greek yogurt

3 tablespoons honey

½ teaspoon ground cinnamon, plus more for garnish

8 tablespoons raspberry jam

16 raspberries (fresh or frozen)

3 tablespoons sliced almonds

1. Line 8 wells of a 24-well mini muffin pan with mini paper muffin cups.

2. In a medium-sized bowl, mix the yogurt, honey, and cinnamon until well combined.

3. Spoon the mixture evenly into the lined cups, putting about 2 tablespoons in each one.

4. Sprinkle a little cinnamon on each cup, then top each one with 1 tablespoon of jam and 2 raspberries. Distribute the almonds evenly among the cups.

5. Freeze for 5 hours or overnight. Allow the bites to soften on the counter for about 5 minutes before removing them from the paper cups. They will keep in the freezer for up to 2 weeks.

ALLERGENS

MIXED FRUIT CANNOLI

OPTION

YIELD: 4 servings **PREP TIME:** 12 minutes

My hometown has the La Festa Italiana festival every year, and that's where I had the best homemade cannoli I've ever tasted. One time, I tried the cannoli with mixed fresh fruit on top, and it changed my life. Here is an easier-to-make version of that cannoli. Use part-skim ricotta in the filling for a lighter treat.

⅔ cup ricotta cheese

¼ cup granulated monk fruit sweetener

1 teaspoon vanilla extract

3 strawberries, diced

¼ mango, diced

¼ cup blueberries, coarsely chopped

4 cannoli shells

6 to 8 fresh mint leaves, torn

Powdered sugar, for garnish (optional)

1. In a medium-sized bowl, mix the ricotta, sweetener, and vanilla until well combined.

2. In a small bowl, gently toss the fruits until evenly distributed.

3. Scoop the ricotta mixture into a food-safe plastic bag. Snip off a corner of the bag and pipe the ricotta filling into the cannoli shells. (Alternatively, you can use a piping bag with a tip if you have one.)

4. Tuck in some fresh mint at either end of the cannoli, then top the ends with the fruit. Dust with powdered sugar before serving, if desired. The cannoli are best served fresh but can last in the fridge for up to 3 days.

ALLERGENS

NOTE: To make this dessert gluten-free, use gluten-free cannoli shells.

MIXED BERRY PIE WONTONS WITH VANILLA PROTEIN YOGURT DIP

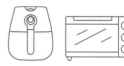

 YIELD: 2 servings   **PREP TIME:** 10 minutes   **COOK TIME:** 8 to 25 minutes, depending on method

If you have leftover wonton wrappers in your fridge, try this simple recipe for a light dessert that's sweet, tart, and fruity. Pairing the berry pie wontons with the vanilla dip makes this treat even more elevated and satisfying. Adding some protein to the dip makes it more balanced and keeps you fuller for longer.

½ cup frozen mixed berries (preferably a mix of blueberries, raspberries, and/or blackberries)

2 tablespoons honey

1 tablespoon cornstarch

6 square wonton wrappers

DIP

¼ cup vanilla-flavored Greek yogurt

2 tablespoons honey

½ scoop vanilla-flavored protein powder (about 2 teaspoons)

¼ teaspoon ground cinnamon, plus more for garnish

ALLERGENS

1. *If using the toaster oven or oven,* preheat it to 375°F.

2. Put the berries in a medium-sized microwave-safe bowl and microwave on high for 30 seconds, or until thawed. Drain the excess liquid.

3. Add the honey and cornstarch to the bowl with the berries and mix until well combined.

4. Place a scant tablespoon of the berry mixture in the center of a wonton wrapper. Dampen the edges of the wrapper with water, fold in all four sides to form a square pouch, and press to seal. Alternatively, you can simply fold one pointed end over to create a triangle.

5. Line the air-fryer basket or a small sheet pan with aluminum foil. Place the wontons in the prepared basket or sheet pan, then coat them with cooking oil spray. Air-fry at 365°F for 8 minutes or bake in the oven for 20 to 25 minutes, until slightly golden brown.

6. Meanwhile, make the dip: Put the yogurt, honey, protein powder, and cinnamon in a small bowl and mix until well combined. Garnish with a light sprinkling of cinnamon.

7. Remove the wontons from the air fryer or oven and allow to cool for a few minutes. Serve with the dip. The wontons are best served fresh but can last in the fridge for up to 3 days. To reheat, microwave on high for 30 seconds.

FUN CHERRIES

   YIELD: 2 servings   **PREP TIME:** 2 minutes, plus 4 hours to soak

Get ready to celebrate another day of being alive with this fun cherry recipe! Feel free to use sparkling wine if you're twenty-one or older. If you haven't reached the legal drinking age or prefer a nonalcoholic version, use sparkling grape juice instead. The sweetness of the cherries and the zing from the sparkling wine or juice marry perfectly in this recipe and will leave you wanting more. Enjoy with caution! Note: This celebratory treat serves two and is meant to be enjoyed as soon as it's made. If you're making it for one person, I suggest you cut the recipe in half.

1 cup fresh cherries with stems

1 cup sparkling wine or sparkling grape juice

1 tablespoon lemon juice

¼ cup granulated monk fruit sweetener

1. Put the cherries in a medium-sized bowl and pour in the sparkling wine or grape juice and lemon juice. Place in the fridge to soak for 4 hours.

2. Use a slotted spoon to transfer the cherries to a serving plate; discard the leftover wine or juice. Immediately sprinkle the cherries with the sweetener and enjoy.

MASON JAR CINNAMON-SPICED VANILLA ICE CREAM

  YIELD: 2 servings   **PREP TIME:** 5 minutes, plus 5 hours to freeze

Don't feel like going out for ice cream? Then make it at home! The best part of this recipe is that you don't need an ice cream maker. All you need are a few simple ingredients and a freezer-safe mason jar—the type with straight sides and a lid. To use this recipe as an all-purpose vanilla ice cream base, simply omit the cinnamon; feel free to add other flavorings of your choice to the base, such as caramel, strawberries, and chocolate.

1 cup heavy cream

¼ cup sweetened condensed milk

3 tablespoons maple syrup

½ teaspoon ground cinnamon

1 teaspoon vanilla extract

Pinch of salt

1. Pour the heavy cream into a freezer-safe 1-pint mason jar. Screw on the lid and shake for 3 minutes, or until slightly thickened and aerated.

2. Add the sweetened condensed milk, maple syrup, cinnamon, vanilla, and salt. Screw on the lid again and shake for another minute, or until the ingredients are well combined.

3. Place the jar in the freezer and freeze for at least 5 hours or overnight.

4. Allow the ice cream to soften slightly on the counter before serving. If your sweet tooth can't wait, microwave it using the defrost setting, checking every 20 seconds, until the ice cream is spoonable. Store in the freezer for up to 1 week.

ALLERGENS

AIR FRYER CARAMEL CHOCOLATE LAVA CAKE

 YIELD: 1 serving   **PREP TIME:** 5 minutes   **COOK TIME:** 11 minutes

This decadent recipe is for those of you who love all things chocolate and caramel. The perfect indulgent dessert to follow a great dinner, it will leave you feeling satisfied and comforted. If you find this cake a little too rich for your liking, pair it with fresh berries and share it with a friend.

¼ cup dark chocolate chips

2 tablespoons refined coconut oil

¼ cup milk of choice

2 tablespoons granulated sugar

½ teaspoon vanilla extract

3 tablespoons all-purpose flour

1 teaspoon cocoa powder

Pinch of salt

1 caramel chew

Powdered sugar, for garnish (optional)

1. Put the chocolate chips and coconut oil in a medium-sized microwave-safe bowl. Microwave on high for 20 seconds, stir, and then microwave for another 20 seconds, or until melted.

2. Mix in the milk, sugar, and vanilla until well combined.

3. Stir in the flour, cocoa powder, and salt until well combined.

4. Coat a 4-ounce ramekin with cooking oil spray and pour the batter into the ramekin. Place the caramel chew in the center and use a spoon to cover the chew with the batter.

5. Place the ramekin in the air-fryer basket and air-fry at 360°F for 10 minutes, or until the top is set around the edges but the center still jiggles slightly when you shake it gently.

6. Dust with powdered sugar, if desired, and enjoy immediately, directly from the ramekin.

ALLERGENS

OPTION

NOTE: To make this cake dairy-free, use vegan chocolate chips and a plant-based milk.

MICROWAVE PEANUT BUTTER & FLUFF MUG CAKE

 YIELD: 1 serving   **PREP TIME:** 5 minutes   **COOK TIME:** 1 minute 30 seconds

Marshmallow fluff and peanut butter pair perfectly in a sandwich, so why not pair them in a mug cake? This filling cake will satisfy your sweet tooth while squashing any hunger pangs. This is the best dessert to eat right before you tuck yourself in for the night. Enjoy it while you're snuggled under your favorite blanket, and you'll have sweet dreams for sure!

1 tablespoon creamy natural peanut butter, plus more for topping

3 tablespoons milk of choice

1 tablespoon vegetable oil

2 tablespoons granulated sugar

½ teaspoon vanilla extract

¼ cup plus 1 tablespoon all-purpose flour

¼ heaping teaspoon baking powder

2 tablespoons marshmallow fluff

1. Put the peanut butter in a microwave-safe 6-ounce bowl or mug and microwave on high for 15 seconds to make it melty. Stir in the milk, vegetable oil, sugar, and vanilla until well combined.

2. Stir in the flour and baking powder.

3. Microwave on high for 1 minute 15 seconds, or until the cake has risen and a toothpick inserted in the center of the cake comes out clean.

4. Top with the marshmallow fluff and a spoonful of peanut butter, then swirl them together with a toothpick. Enjoy immediately, directly from the bowl or mug.

ALLERGENS

OPTION

NOTE: To make this cake dairy-free, use a plant-based milk.

HANDY-DANDY CANDY BARS

  YIELD: 2 candy bars **PREP TIME:** 10 minutes, plus 50 minutes to freeze
COOK TIME: 1 minute

Candy bars are one of the top sweet treats, and for good reason. They are portable and can last a long time without spoiling. While this candy bar won't keep as long as the store-bought equivalent, it will last for weeks without going bad, you don't need to refrigerate it, and it's great for a grab-and-go snack. If you want more protein to keep you feeling satisfied for longer, add some protein powder to the filling.

FILLING

⅔ **cup unsweetened shredded coconut**

3 **tablespoons sliced almonds, coarsely chopped, plus more for garnish**

3 **tablespoons honey**

½ **teaspoon vanilla extract**

½ **teaspoon ground cinnamon**

COATING

½ **cup dark chocolate chips**

1 **tablespoon refined coconut oil**

Pinch of salt, for garnish

1. Line a small sheet pan or other food-safe tray with parchment paper. In a medium-sized bowl, mix the coconut, chopped almonds, honey, vanilla, and cinnamon until well combined. Once mixed, mold the filling into two 2 by ½-inch rectangles and place on the lined tray. Place in the freezer for 40 minutes.

2. Put the chocolate chips and coconut oil in a small microwave-safe bowl. Microwave on high for 1 minute, or until melted, stirring every 20 seconds.

3. Using a fork, dip the frozen coconut filling into the melted chocolate and until it's evenly coated on all sides. Place the chocolate-coated candy bar on the prepared pan. Repeat with the second rectangle of frozen coconut filling. If the melted chocolate has begun to solidify, microwave it on high for another 20 seconds.

4. Sprinkle the candy bars with the salt and some sliced almonds. Freeze for another 10 minutes.

5. Store on the counter for up to 1 week or in the fridge for up to 2 weeks.

NOTE: To make these candy bars dairy-free, use vegan chocolate chips.

STRAWBERRIES & CREAM COOKIE DOUGH

 YIELD: 2 servings   **PREP TIME:** 5 minutes   **COOK TIME:** 1 minute 30 seconds

Cookie dough has always been one of my go-to desserts. It's so easy to make, and you don't need to wait for baking. Unlike traditional cookie dough recipes, this raw dough uses heat-treated flour and doesn't include egg, so you don't need to worry about salmonella or *E. coli*. I prefer to use freeze-dried strawberries here for their texture, but if you can't find them, fresh berries work too.

½ cup all-purpose flour

⅓ cup brown sugar

1 tablespoon granulated sugar

Pinch of salt

¼ cup (½ stick) unsalted butter, softened

1 tablespoon milk of choice

½ teaspoon vanilla extract

3 tablespoons chopped white chocolate

3 tablespoons freeze-dried or diced fresh strawberries

1. Heat-treat the flour by spreading it on a medium-sized microwave-safe plate and microwaving on high for 1 minute 30 seconds, stirring every 30 seconds. Use an instant-read thermometer to make sure the temperature of the flour has reached 165°F.

2. Transfer the heat-treated flour to a medium-sized bowl and allow to cool to room temperature, then mix in the brown sugar, granulated sugar, salt, butter, milk, and vanilla until well combined.

3. Fold in the white chocolate and strawberries. The dough is best served fresh but can last in the fridge for up to 2 days if using fresh strawberries or up to 4 days if using freeze-dried strawberries.

ALLERGENS

FURTHER READING

The following articles are excellent resources for learning more about creating good eating habits for a balanced diet:

"A Balanced Diet":
www.healthdirect.gov.au/balanced-diet

"A Balanced Diet":
www.researchgate.net/publication/281455815_Balanced_Diet

"Eating a Balanced Diet: A Healthy Life Through a Balanced Diet in the Age of Longevity":
www.pubmed.ncbi.nlm.nih.gov/31089539/

"Eating to Boost Energy":
www.eatright.org/health/wellness/healthful-habits/eating-to-boost-energy

"Healthy Eating Plate":
www.hsph.harvard.edu/nutritionsource/healthy-eating-plate

"Putting the Balance in a Balanced Diet":
www.health.harvard.edu/nutrition/putting-the-balance-in-a-balanced-diet/

RECIPE INDEX

SIMPLE BREAKFASTS

EFFORTLESS LUNCHES

SATISFYING SNACKIES

 124
Roasted Tomato & Feta Cheese Dip

 126
Pepperoni Pizza Sticks

 128
Air Fryer Parmesan Garlic Carrot Fries

 130
Sweet Potato Chips

 132
Air Fryer BBQ Potato Skin Snackers

 134
Slow Cooker Chicken Enchilada Dip

 136
2-Ingredient Pepperoni Cheese Bites

 138
Veggie & Ricotta–Stuffed Portabella Mushrooms

 140
Roasted Tomato & Herbed Ricotta Toast

 142
Baked Jalapeño, Raspberry & Cream Cheese Dip

 144
Slow Cooker Spinach Artichoke Dip

EASY-PEASY DINNERS

Dinners in a Dash

 148
Polenta Pie

 150
Microwave Buffalo Chicken Mac & Cheese

 152
Air Fryer Crab Cakes

 154
Chicken & Potato Goulash

 156
Pizza Quesadilla

 158
Sheet Pan Sausage, Peppers & Gnocchi with Hot Honey Sauce

 160
Smoky Cheese-Stuffed Chicken with Broccoli

 162
Cabbage Rolls with Spicy Soy Dipping Sauce

 164
Air Fryer Shrimp Kabobs

 166
Cheesy Garlicky Spaghetti Squash

 168
Roasted Red Pepper Salmon & Green Beans

 170
Chili Honey–Glazed Salmon & Broccoli

 172
Cod & Brie with Spicy Sauce

 174
Parmesan-Crusted Tilapia & Asparagus

 176
Sheet Pan Chicken & Broccoli

 178
One-Pot Creamy Tomato Pasta

 180
Hidden Veggie Pasta

Slow and Steady Suppers

 182
Healing Chicken Noodle Soup

 184
Soul-Warming Ham & Potato Soup

 186
Creamy Tortellini Soup

 188
Hearty Turkey Chili

 190
Comforting Winter Soup

 192
BBQ Pulled Chicken Sandwiches

 194
Chicken Tikka Masala

 196
Tavern Pot Roast

 198
Garlic Chicken Parm Pasta

 200
Classic Sloppy Joes

 202
Birria Tacos

SWEET TREATS

Quick Fixes

 206
Cookies & Cream Frozen Yogurt

 208
Frozen Blueberry & Nut Clusters

 210
Cinnamon Sugar Pie Crusties

 212
Brown Sugar Toast Bites

 214
Chocolate Protein Cheesecake Dip

 216
Creamy Vanilla Double Protein Dip

 218
Date Caramel Dip

 220
Bitchin' Bark

 222
Raspberry-Filled Frozen Yogurt Bites

Indulgent Treats

 224
Mixed Fruit Cannoli

 226
Mixed Berry Pie Wontons with Vanilla Protein Yogurt Dip

 228
Fun Cherries

 230
Mason Jar Cinnamon-Spiced Vanilla Ice Cream

 232
Air Fryer Caramel Chocolate Lava Cake

 234
Microwave Peanut Butter & Fluff Mug Cake

 236
Handy-Dandy Candy Bars

 238
Strawberries & Cream Cookie Dough

GENERAL INDEX